♥GRANDMA♥

from

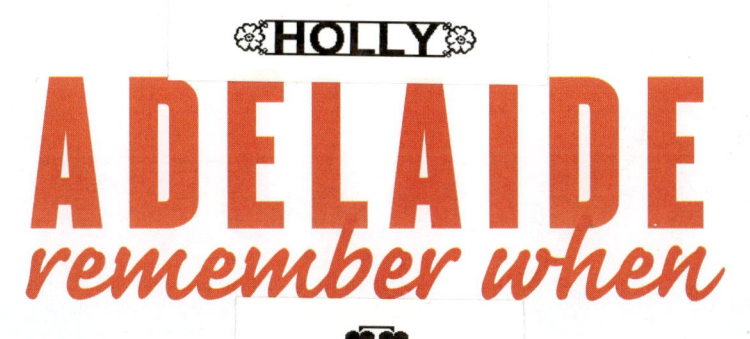

♥RUTH♥

❀HOLLY❀

# ADELAIDE
*remember when*

♥SIMON♥

♥SUMMER♥

Bob Byrne had a long career in commercial radio, particularly 5DN Adelaide, before becoming a columnist/blogger at *The Adelaide Advertiser*, writing about Adelaide of the recent past. He set up the popular 'Adelaide Remember When' Facebook page, the inspiration for this book.

*State Library of South Australia zperi13972704,
courtesy of Adelaide Festival Corporation*

# ADELAIDE
*remember when*

## BOB BYRNE

NEWSOUTH

# A NOTE FROM BOB

My sincere thanks to the many people who have contributed to this book, to all those who have allowed me to use photos from their personal collections, and to those who have contributed their own memories from the Baby Boomer years.

Growing up in the 1950s through to the '80s, we were perhaps the last generation to walk or ride our bikes to school. We climbed trees, skinned our knees and elbows, played in the street with all the other neighbourhood kids until the street lights went on. On a hot Adelaide summer night we slept outside on the lawn or at the beach, hoping to catch a cool breeze. We could walk out the front door and leave it unlocked and we never bothered about padlocking the bicycle. Everybody's mum was home after school and we got a clip around the ear when we'd been naughty. We were the generation that gave the world rock'n'roll music, the sexual revolution of the 1960s and the social revolution of the 1970s.

Come with me on a trip down 'Memory Lane' as we recall that era again through the words and photos on these pages.

*The author in the 1970s*

# FOREWORD

This is a book for everyone: a contemporary history of Adelaide chiefly from the 1950s through to an era that predominately belongs to the Baby Boomer generation, as well as a nostalgic stroll down memory lane for those of us who shared the times. For younger South Australians these fascinating photos give a glimpse into bygone days.

Memories are moments that leave indelible footprints in our mind – they engender a myriad of feelings. Mostly they make us feel sentimental about the good times and the people, places and events that shaped our lives.

'Adelaide Remember When' had its beginning when former radio personality Bob Byrne (5KA, 5AD, 5DN) first uploaded a few old photos to his website in 2013. Public interest was instant. As a result Bob developed a dedicated Facebook page that continues to grow in popularity. A natural extension is this beautiful book of lost treasures reflecting how we were back then. It is a pictorial reminder of beach pavilions, ballrooms and stately old buildings, department stores, the legendary pie cart, the city's equally legendary personalities, games we played as kids, family cars, old trams, magic moments in sport, pop hysteria, the early days of television and wireless, the famous 5AD Top 40 Chart and so much more.

A respected broadcaster in Adelaide for over three decades, Bob Byrne continues to work in media at *The Advertiser*. By compiling this engaging book, Bob, together with his Facebook contributors, has given readers the pleasure of reminiscing and recapturing a fascinating past.

Today Adelaide is deservedly named as one of the world's most livable cities. It is a charming place to call home: contemporary, creative, elegant and easy for those seeking a comfortable and enviable way of life. While these pages reflect considerable changes over the years and sadly the loss of some stunning buildings along the way, the city continues to evolve with style and is a special place to be cherished and enjoyed.

*Sue Fraser Mapp*
*Friend and former radio colleague*

# 1995 ADELAIDE

*The glorious days of the Adelaide Grand Prix continued for 10 years. In this photo Damon Hill is winning the 1995 Grand prix on the famous street circuit*

*Photo by News Ltd/Newspix*

There was a magical feeling in the air in Adelaide in late 1985 as the first Adelaide Grand Prix roared to life.

That early November day was the culmination of years of planning and hard work going back to the early 1980s when businessman Bill O'Gorman originally came up with the idea of hosting a Formula One race to try to do something to improve the city's image.

South Australia's Premier John Bannon immediately got behind the idea and O'Gorman flew to London to do a deal with F1 boss Bernie Ecclestone. The result of the meeting was a seven-year contract, starting in 1985, to stage the F1 in Australia.

Dr Mal Hemmerling, a senior civil servant, was put in charge and it was decided to build the street circuit incorporating Victoria Park with a long straight on Dequetteville Terrace.

It proved a winner immediately with the drivers proclaiming it as the best street circuit in Formula One racing. The street circuit wasn't the only winner for Adelaide.

The teams soon discovered how friendly the city was, helped by the fact that the first race was an end-of-season event after the World Championship had been settled.

It established the tradition then of Adelaide being just one big party. And we loved it!

# #1 FACT

Adelaide Writers' Week was Australia's first literary festival, is internationally acclaimed and attracts talent from around the world of publishing. It started in 1960 and has been going strong ever since in the Pioneer Women's Memorial Garden. It forms part of the Adelaide Festival of the Arts.

1955

Once you put the pennies in, they stayed in. There was no way to get the money out until you took your full money box to the bank and they'd swap it for a new one

*ARW*

Remember when pocket money was something that had to be earned and never given freely?

Most parents in the 1950s and 1960s were frugal and after all the household bills were paid from the single-income pay packet, I imagine there would not have been a lot left. One of my wife's pocket-money jobs was to regularly wash and clean the hairbrushes at home. As boys we seemed to have more freedom than the girls, which allowed us to scout around most weekends looking for soft-drink bottles, which we'd take back to the corner shop for the deposit, press button B in all the public phone boxes, or even try to catch some fish for which mum might give a shilling or two.

I know that some kids today still have to do chores to get their pocket money but for us it was never guaranteed, you did the chores and hoped you might get paid.

# 1959

The State-heritage listed Bank of New South Wales building on the corner of King William Street and North Terrace, has been given a new lease of life in 2014 as the Jamie Oliver Italian Restaurant in Adelaide.

The Bank of New South Wales building at mid century

*Max Dupain, courtesy of National Archives of Australia: A1200,L7482*

The building, constructed during World War II, had stood unused since 2006. When plans were announced in 2013 for a new use for the building, the president of the National Trust in South Australia, Professor Norman Etherington said: 'We can only applaud when someone finds a new use for a valuable building'. Heritage approval was given for two windows facing King William Street to be extended down to near street level.

1964

Italian fare: pizza and spaghetti washed down with a cappuccino make the perfect lunch at Marina Pizza Bar on Hindley Street, 1964

*Photo by Pat Crowe/Newspix*

The Marina Pizza Bar opened in 1964 on the south-western corner of Hindley and Morphett Streets, two years before Marcellina's and was the first pizza bar in the city. Marina's sold pizza for 35c, and a bowl of spaghetti for 25c. It was at the same location for 10 years before the building was demolished to make way for road-widening works. It was established by Italian immigrants Mario Bellati and his wife Amelia. According to their son Walter, Marina's was a real coffee shop with Italian food. 'We were the only place in Hindley Street you could go to get a meal at midnight or 1am.' Walter says his dad experimented with all sorts of pizza toppings and was pretty upset when their chef went to Marcellina's when they opened in 1966.

1950

Victoria Square, 1950. Why did it look much bigger back then?

*State Library of South Australia B63137*

1950

This is Victoria Square on a wet Adelaide day in 1950. I can't remember back that far myself, but obviously King William Street ran straight through the square then and it looks as though Queen Victoria was on an island in the middle of the road. The original caption points out the 'shaped lawns and flower beds where pedestrians walk near the traffic of trams and motor cars'. And of course the public toilets are there. From memory it used to cost a penny to go to those lavatories and they had an attendant who would give you a small towel after you washed your hands. And look, there don't appear to be traffic lights!

# 1958

Samorn was a great favourite at the zoo and our last elephant. In *Elephant in our Zoo*, a collection of short stories about Samorn who arrived here in 1956 as a royal gift to Adelaide from the King of Siam, Victoria Raine writes:

> Right from the start she was bright, very observant, curious, and rarely forgot. She formed many staff friends and became very attached to Hero Nuus, her senior keeper, who effectively became her 'mahout'. She was a jealous, working, clever and trustworthy elephant both up front and behind the scenes, and would not share her beloved jobs.

Samorn stopped giving rides in 1982 and was moved to Monarto Zoo in 1991. She died in 1994.

A day out at the Adelaide Zoo always included a ride in the elephant cart pulled by Samorn. Here she is at work in 1958

*Photo by News Ltd/Newspix*

Remember the dirt-spattered days of Adelaide's ace suburban motorsport venue?

*Courtesy of Noel O'Connor*

1975

Rowley Park was a huge part of Adelaide during the summer months throughout the 1950s, 1960s and up until 1979 when it was closed. In its heyday Rowley Park, or the 'Pughole' as it was nicknamed, would attract up to 15,000 fans every Friday night with champion drivers like Kym Bonython, Jack Scott, the great Bob Tattersall, Bill Wigzell and Ray Skipper. There was the smell of burning rubber and exhaust fumes, the sound of screeching tyres, with mud flying everywhere as the cars raced around the track at breakneck speed. All of Adelaide knew the slogan 'Friday Night is Speedway Night' and almost everyone can still recall the cartoon showing a big crowd, including a jockey, a grandmother and a heavily bandaged patient on a stretcher, all off to the Friday night speedway. What tremendous fun it was with regular smashes and crashes and the annual Demolition Derby, which would run for over an hour.

I sometimes pass the housing estate where Rowley Park used to be on Torrens Road, Brompton, and I'm immediately taken back to those balmy summer nights with the huge crowds cheering, the cars flying around the track, the noise and the sheer excitement of the speedway.

Kym Bonython cuts a dashing figure on two wheels

*Photo by News Ltd/Newspix*

# 1978

On the steps of State Parliament after a protest rally and march, tempers flared over the sacking of Police Commissioner Harold Salisbury

*Photo by News Ltd/Newspix*

On 17 January 1978 the South Australian Police Commissioner, Harold Salisbury, was dismissed by the State Government under Premier Don Dunstan.

The sacking caused a furore but Dunstan refused to back down, claiming that Mr Salisbury had 'so misled the Government that wrong information was given to Parliament and the people'. It was also claimed that Special Branch held files on a large number of people not convicted of any offence. An enquiry was conducted by the South Australian Supreme Court and it was found that, while there were files on persons and organisations 'reasonably suspected of being potential security risks', there were also records relating to matters, persons and organisations 'having no connection whatsoever with genuine security risks'.

The sacking sparked public outrage with 10,000 members of the public and police officers attending a protest rally in Victoria Square. A subsequent royal commission chaired by Justice Roma Mitchell vindicated the government decision, finding that answers provided by Mr Salisbury to the government were 'inaccurate by omission'. Mr Salisbury returned to England and died in 1991.

1911

The beautiful old Theatre Royal in Hindley Street had the honour of showing the first moving pictures in Adelaide and there were two open-air theatres: this one in Victoria Square and the other on North Terrace.

Adelaide's 'Outdoor Picture Theatre' in Victoria Square in 1911. In the foreground is Best's Pictures, an open-air picture theatre. Moore's Department Store is on the left

*State Library of South Australia B2187*

15

1962

1962

Birks Department Store in Rundle Street was built around the 1920s and remained a major force in retailing in Adelaide up until it was sold in 1954 to the David Jones Group from Sydney. It continued to trade under the name Birks until the early 1960s when the building was demolished and David Jones built their showroom on the site.

Charles Birks Department Store taken from the Oriental Hotel on the corner of Gawler Place

*Frank Hall, courtesy of Elaine Hall*

# 1933

Dear old 'Johnnies'. John Martin's was an Adelaide icon that first opened its doors in 1866 and after 132 years of trading in Rundle Street and later Rundle Mall, closed in 1998. The Hayward family owned and operated the business for most of that time and were responsible for introducing two other Adelaide icons: the Christmas Pageant and the Magic Cave.

The Haywards lived in Adelaide and through the company had a strong sense of civic duty, both to their staff and the South Australian community, sponsoring sports teams, the Adelaide leg of The Beatles Australian tour and supporting many charities and other worthwhile causes.

The official opening of Adelaide's first elevator at John Martin's in 1933

*Photo by News Ltd/Newspix*

1960

# #2
## FACT

Coopers has been producing refreshing ales and dark stouts for over 150 years, since 1862. It is wholly Australian owned and is still run by descendants of the founder, Thomas Cooper. You can book a tour round the Regency Park brewery.

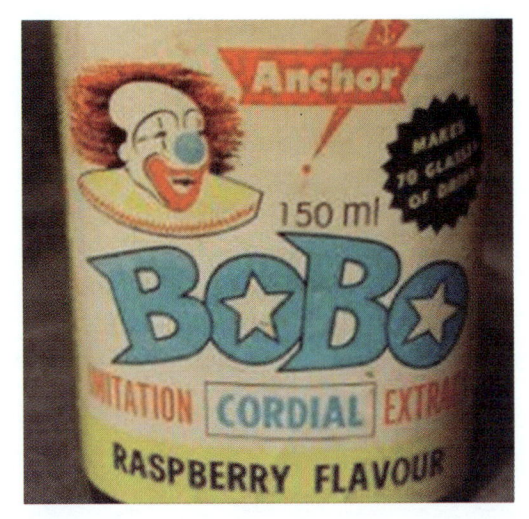

When you were thirsty as a kid, there was only one choice

*Courtesy of Nick Haines*

Bobo Cordial was a cordial concentrate that needed to be mixed with copious quantities of sugar and water. For those too impatient to wait for Mum to mix the correct ingredients, a rude shock awaited! The concentrate was very strong, which was nothing like the taste of the final mixture.

Bobo of course was the famous clown from NWS Channel 9 and was a star of the Channel Niners and other kids programs back in the 1960s, later moving to Channel 10. In those early days of TV in Adelaide, there were many locally produced TV shows with local, well-known personalities, and many products were branded to take advantage of their popularity. Alas most of our TV shows are now produced in either Sydney or Melbourne and very little on-air content is made in 'smaller' markets such as Adelaide.

## 1970

Anne Wills, best known to Adelaide TV audiences as 'Willsy', started her career as the weather girl on Channel 9 back in 1965. It wasn't long however before her natural talents were recognised and she was making regular appearances on *Adelaide Tonight* variety show with Ernie Sigley and Lionel Williams. She also presented and appeared on many other locally based Channel 9 TV programs, including *AM Adelaide*. She later moved to Channel 7, also as a weather presenter on *7 Nightly News* and made regular appearances on Adelaide radio, including co-hosting the 5DN *Breakfast Show* with Geoff Sunderland. Anne has been part of the Adelaide entertainment scene for many years and during that time has won a total of 19 Logies, an Australian record.

Anne Wills entertaining the 1st Australian Task Force at Nui Dat's Luscombe Bowl as part of the army-sponsored concert in Vietnam in 1970

*Photo by News Ltd/Newspix*

1970

1963

Dawn Crocker and Douglas McCallum, both aged 8, bouncing around on their pogo sticks, watched by other students at Mitcham Primary School in 1963

*Photo by News Ltd/Newspix*

**1950**

**HAVE AN Alaska ICE CREAM ESKIMO PIE**

**CHOCOLATE COATED... The Food That's Fun**

Swimming in the Torrens, playing out in the street with all the other kids until all hours and riding our bikes from one end of town to another were just some of the games we played in the 1950s, '60s and '70s. If you could scrounge a couple of old jam tins and a couple of pieces of string, you could make a pair of stilts. Maybe your parents bought a pair of rollerskates that would lace up over your shoes, or a pogo stick. There weren't too many pogo sticks in our neighbourhood due to the expense, but they were definitely a toy of the '60s! It's no wonder kids were so skinny then, just imagine how much energy it took to bounce around on a pogo stick for 10 minutes!

Before the fast food craze, we used to get a hamburger at the Blue & White Cafe in O'Connell Street or at Burger King on Anzac Highway, slurp a milkshake at Sigalas in Rundle Street and cool off with an Adelaide-made ice-cream from Amscol or Alaska

*State Library of South Australia, eposter b215544645*

Records indicate that the Alaska Ice Cream and Produce Company commenced business at Thebarton in 1921. Alaska was another ice-cream favourite in Adelaide while we were growing up. I guess most people will remember Alaska Eskimo Pies, a chocolate-coated ice-cream in a silver foil wrapper. The old Alaska Ice Cream Factory in Thebarton was built around 1950 and is now called Alaska Towers and is within the University Research Park.

## 1964

The first post on 'Adelaide Remember When' appeared after I had been listening to a radio interview on the ABC with Ron Tremaine, in which he repeated the story of how the Beatles came to Adelaide.

Ron talked about his meeting with Ken Brodziak (who brought the Beatles to Australia), and how Adelaide had not been included in the original tour. Ron was something of an entrepreneur and approached John Martins Department Store to sponsor a visit to Adelaide by the Fab Four, then enlisted the help of his good friend and number one DJ in town, Bob Francis. Jim Slade, another popular DJ on 5KA, also joined in and between them they got 80,000 signatures on a petition that Ron presented to Mr Brodziak to get the Beatles here. It worked, and on 12 June 1964 the Beatles arrived to the greatest reception they had yet received anywhere in the world.

The visit brought the city to a standstill when over 300,000 fans turned out to welcome the group.

I posted the story and to my amazement, some of my own Facebook friends re-posted it and within 24 hours it had received over a thousand views and a hundred likes. I decided to do a few more posts, which also received likes and comments and shares and so I decided to keep on with the website and post each day.

When the Beatles arrived in Adelaide in 1964 the scene outside the Town Hall was absolute mayhem

*Photo by News Ltd/Newspix*

1964

# 1985

The Compass Cup has drawn wide publicity for Mount Compass and the Fleurieu Peninsula ever since the first race in 1974. As an annual event it raises money for charity each year and is a great fun day out, known to most Adelaideans.

Lyn Mallett explains how the Cup began:

> My father, Bill Epps, was the creator of the Compass Cup. It all began on our farm 'Goonamurra' in Mount Compass when he called one morning to the house cow, who was down the far paddock. Old Bet heard the call and came charging up to the shed, and the seed was sown: a cow race! What was to be a one-off to raise money by the local Rural Youth Club and St Mary's orphanage, has now become a South Australian staple.

At the 1985 Compass Cup radio and TV personality Scott McBain adopted an unorthodox style on his mount, Desira-Bull

*Photo by News Ltd/Newspix*

1972

South Australia's most colourful, controversial and enlightened pollie ever has to be Don Dunstan. He was twice Premier of South Australia, in 1967 and 1968 and then again from 1970 to 1979. Dunstan brought about many changes to the State in what became known as 'The Dunstan Era'. Under his leadership we saw the recognition of Aboriginal land rights, the abolition of the death penalty and the decriminalisation of homosexuality. He was also the prime mover of anti-discrimination legislation and pushed for the relaxation of both censorship and drinking laws. It was during his years as Premier that the Rundle Mall was established, along with the Adelaide Festival Centre and the South Australian Film Corporation. Whether it was turning up in Parliament in pink shorts, sacking police commissioners, turning back the tide at Glenelg Beach in 1976, introducing major changes to just about everything, he could always grab a headline!

Don Dunstan in his famous pink shorts

*Photo by News Ltd/Newspix*

Kids jumping off the weir and swimming in the Torrens, 1962

*Photo by Dick Hewett/Newspix*

1962

First produced in 1948, FruChocs have been declared by the National Trust as having 'cultural and historical significance to the state of South Australia'

*Courtesy of Robern Menz*

It's hard to imagine that even up to the late 1960s kids used to swim in the Torrens. In fact I remember before the days of the family car, private backyard swimming pools and the rubbish that now pollutes the Torrens, the river was the only place to have a swim in summer if you lived anywhere near the city or in some of the suburban areas that the Torrens passed through.

There are plans to clean up the Torrens with the Federal Government promising to spend money on getting rid of the algal problems that have plagued the river for years, on bank stabilisation, weed eradication and re-vegetation.

I won't hold my breath, but we can all live in hope!

# #3
FACT

The Glenelg Tram runs for 15 kilometres from the Adelaide Entertainment Centre in Hindmarsh through Victoria Square and the centre of the city to Jetty Road and popular Glenelg Beach. It is the only tramway left in Adelaide.

# 1966

Police and searchers wade through the Patawalonga during the search for the missing children in January 1966

*Photo by News Ltd/Newspix*

The missing Beaumont children head this edition of *The Advertiser*

*Photo by News Ltd/Newspix*

After Australia Day 1966, Adelaide changed forever. On that day the Beaumont children – Jane, Arnna and Grant – disappeared from Glenelg beach and were never found. The case resulted in one of the largest police investigations in Australian criminal history and remains one of the most baffling and infamous cold cases.

A massive search was launched by police and volunteers, scouring the coast

1966

for kilometres both north and south of the Colley Reserve, in the hope of finding a clue. By the weekend the disappearance of the Beaumont children was a national news item and the search had become one of the biggest ever mounted in Australia. It was extended to every seaside suburb, and beyond. Sandhills were searched, and police knocked on the door of every house that the children could have passed on their way home. Hundreds of ordinary citizens asked if there was any way in which they could help as almost the entire city became involved in the hunt.

The drama even involved international psychic Gerard Croiset and later his son as authorities continued to try and crack the case. Many parents changed the way they supervised their children on a daily basis after the disappearances and the case led many to conclude that Adelaide had a dark and evil underbelly.

1972

The Cactus Ranch was on the old Port Wakefield Road when it was a single-lane highway. Later the highway moved away from the ranch and it's now fallen into a state of disrepair

*Courtesy of Diana Field*

You knew you were getting close to Adelaide when you passed the Arizona Cactus Ranch on Port Wakefield Road. Lots of people used to stop there to break their journey and admire the cacti.

Matt Walsh with his mother and grandparents. The cacti were amazing, but how about the rock work?

*Courtesy of Matt Walsh*

1958

Glenelg Migrant Hostel where John D'Arcy lived on arrival from England

*Migration Museum Photographic Collection (8659685046), courtesy Barbara Reis*

There were migrant hostels in Glenelg, Gepps Cross, Elder Park, Gawler, Hendon, Mallala, Pennington/Finsbury, Rosewater, Salisbury, Semaphore, Smithfield, Woodside, Woodville and several in country centres. The hostels were temporary homes for a large number of migrants, from people displaced through World War II, and refugees, through to 'Ten Pound Poms'. Most hostels opened in the late 1940s and early '50s and closed by the mid to late '70s. Many of us went to school with kids who lived for a period of time in the hostels.

The founding guitarist of popular local band ZOOT, John D'Arcy had left England with his family and lived at Glenelg Migrant Hostels, and went to Plympton High School, where he met Beeb Birtles. Beeb Birtles is well known to many Adelaideans as a leading member of band ZOOT, and as founding member of one of the greatest bands ever to play on the worldstage in the 1970s and early '80s: 'Little River Band'.

33

# 1981

Remember Baz and Pilko on Adelaide radio at breakfast time in the '70s and '80s? Along with Peter Plus they were compulsory listening and at one stage in the late '70s almost one radio in every two was tuned in for their zany antics on the air.

Legend has it that the first time they worked together was on the panel at Channel 7 for the Good Friday Appeal. Prior to that they had both been working at 5AD, but on separate programs. It was a partnership that would last for decades.

In November 1982 they were the highest-rating radio show in Australia and in 1984 when they moved to Sydney it was front page local news. They achieved local legend status and Radio 5AD became the city's number one radio station, spearheaded by their show.

Baz and Pilko celebrate another ratings win in 1981

*Photo by News Ltd/Newspix*

Neighbourhood kids playing street cricket in Tomsey Court in the city in 1966

*Photo by News Ltd/Newspix*

1966

I often ask people, what is the thing they most remember about growing up in Adelaide and suburbs from about the 1950s to the 1980s and quite often it will be the really simple things: a game of footy or cricket in the street with all the neighbourhood kids; sleeping out on the lawn on a really hot summer night; leaving the house unlocked while you ducked down the street; riding your bike all over the place on a weekend and never having to worry that it would be pinched; and playing outside until the street lights came on and it was tea time!

## 1990

Red Hen railcars bring back some rather special memories of Adelaide. They were first introduced in the late 1950s and continued operating right through until the early 1990s, running to all local stations. Red Hens were painted a distinctive red colour, with a dull grey interior and vinyl seating. They were far from glamorous and had no air-conditioning system. Almost anyone who travelled by rail in those days will recall that the only way to get cool air on a hot Adelaide summer's day was to hold the doors open as the train sped through the suburbs, a practice that would be frowned on today, but somehow was allowed back then.

The first Red Hens were built locally at Islington Railway Workshops and were introduced to replace the old suburban steam trains. This train is passing Eden Hills in 1990

*Wikimedia, courtesy of Ian Threlfall*

2004

Who can forget Port Adelaide's grand final flag in 2004? A great and memorable moment for the Cornes brothers, Kane and Chad

Photo by News Ltd/Newspix

Port Adelaide celebrated its first AFL Premiership in 2004 under coach Mark Williams. Port beat Brisbane that year after finals disappointments and being labelled as a team of chokers. The coach famously grabbed his tie and simulated being choked on national TV as his team celebrated with a lap of honour to soak up the moment.

37

# 1966

Remember how we would visit the local dump, ride there on our bikes and scour the pile of rubbish looking for a set of wheels on an axle? Old pram wheels were generally the best, and sometimes would be very hard to find. To own two sets of pram wheels was priceless because it was then just a matter of finding a length of timber, an apple crate for the seat, a bolt to attach the 'steerable' front wheels and a piece of rope with which to steer, put it all together and then find the steepest hill and go careering down it at breakneck speed!

There were lots of skinned knees and elbows, gravel rash and torn clothes. I can recall one of my friend's sisters was a bit of a tomboy and would go right to the top of the hill, daring me and my boyhood mates to go faster all the time. Sometimes that ended in tears.

Incidentally, no crash helmets (who could afford to buy one of those?), no elbow or knee pads. How on earth did we survive some of those games?

Urged on by friends, Terry Gifford, 12, of Hove is airborne in his billycart at Seacliff in 1966

*Photo by Pat Crowe/Newspix*

# #4
## FACT

Adelaide is a city of festivals. There is the Adelaide Festival of the Arts, Writers Week, Adelaide Fringe, WOMADelaide, Feast Festival, Cabaret Festival, Film Festival, Sala Festival, Come Out Festival, Adelaide International Guitar Festival, OzAsia Festival and many more. Take your pick!

1970

One of Adelaide's most-loved radio personalities in the '60's, '70s and '80s was John Vincent. I worked with 'Vinnie' between 1970 and 1972 at 5AD and he was the most generous, kind, funny and genuine person you could ever meet.

Growing up and living in Adelaide in that '60s to '80s era, you would have at some time heard him on air, seen him on TV, attended a dance where he was compere or bought one of his Ken Oath records or cassettes. John spent time 'on-air' at 5AD, 5KA and SAFM. He died in 2009 and, in a wonderful tribute to how much he was loved and respected, over 500 people attended his funeral.

One of the true greats of Adelaide in 'our' era.

John Vincent, circa 1970
*Photo by News Ltd/Newspix*

## 1972

The Bowman Building and Arcade was on King William Street near Currie Street and had numerous shops and offices, including a record shop owned by Kym Bonython. The building was erected by Keith Bowman in the early 20th century, was five-storeys high and was described as 'an early example of reinforced concrete in multi-storey architecture'. It was demolished in 1972. Another beautiful old building that we have lost.

Bowman Building and Arcade was on King William Street

*Frank Hall, courtesy of Elaine Hall*

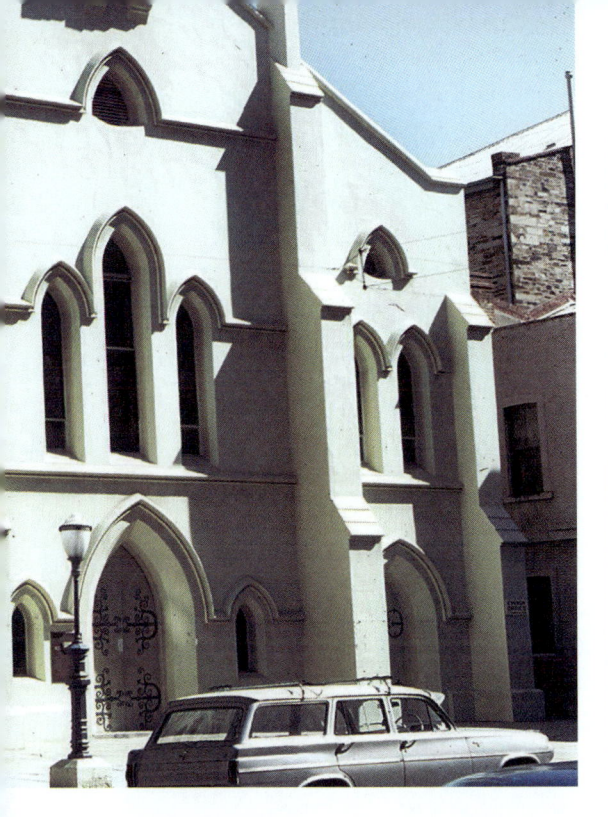

## 1976

Pirie Street Methodist Church, where Elaine Hall's parents married in 1939

*Frank Hall, courtesy of Elaine Hall*

Gary Meadows was well known to Adelaideans as the host of the Channel 10 Christmas Appeal. From left, SAS 10 personality Noel O'Connor, Fat Cat (when he was a grey cat – pre colour TV), Debbie Clark, Rock Wallaby and Gary

*Courtesy of Noel O'Connor*

The Pirie Street Methodist Church, located behind the Adelaide Town Hall, was the 'cathedral church' of Methodism in Adelaide. It was built in 1850, it could seat 800 downstairs, and an additional 400 in the galleries. In 1969 Pirie Street Methodist congregation merged with nearby Stow Congregational Church, an early step in what was to become the Uniting Church.

In 1972 the church was closed and demolished to make way for the Colonel Light Centre.

Gary Meadows was a radio and TV personality, originally from Perth, but through appearances on national TV shows like *The Price is Right*, he captured a large and devoted following around Australia.

He was best known and remembered in Adelaide as host of the Channel 10 Christmas Appeal, which brought the stars of the network together from all around the country. Gary worked tirelessly on the show and could often be seen openly weeping as he would talk to some of the children affected by illness. He died in 1982 at the young age of 43 from a heart attack.

1 9 7 9

# 1979

The 'Adventure Playground' at Monash will bring back a lot of happy memories for many Adelaide families. It was started in the late 1960s by engineer Grant Telfer and was developed over a twenty-year period at an estimated cost of $150,000. Thousands of children and adults swarmed to the park, near Berri, every year.

Adelaideans used to go camping in the Riverland during the school holidays and a highlight of the trip was the day spent in the free playground with its giant spiral slides, see-saws, flying foxes, fun slides and roller coaster. Much of the play equipment was made from scrap metal, was cleverly designed and offered something different to the standard children's playground.

Despite its immense popularity the park was closed in 1992 due to insurance and injury claims. Another safer version of the park has since re-opened.

Monash Adventure Playground, 1979. Much of the original equipment was later deemed to be unsafe by authorities

*Photo by News Ltd/Newspix*

## 1953

*The Green and Gold Cookery Book* was started as a fund raiser for King's College (now Pembroke). It was first published in 1923. The school community and others contributed recipes, household and laundry hints, remedies and other miscellaneous information.

I remember my mother using her *Green and Gold Cookery Book* whenever she was cooking a cake or any recipe where she needed a bit of guidance. It was probably as well-used as the one below. The 90th edition has just been published.

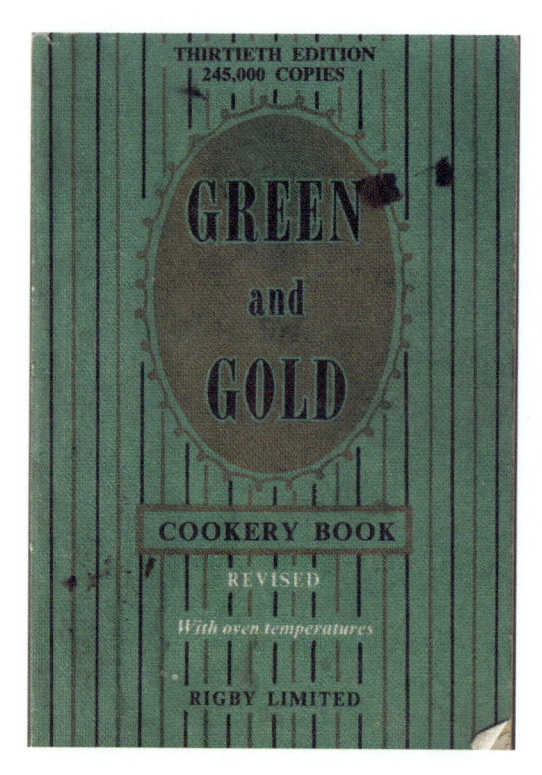

The old *Green and Gold* cookbook – passed on from mother to daughter. The 30th edition was published in 1953

*Courtesy of Lorraine Clarbull*

Glenelg Beach Quest, 1954. The girls were judged on beauty, poise, charm, deportment, manner, diction and open air sports activities

*Photo by News Ltd/Newspix*

1954

**SUNDAY ADVERTISER BEACH GIRL QUEST ERE TODAY at 3 P.M**

The 1954 Beach Girl Quest at Glenelg attracted a crowd of some 25,000 people! Entrants to the quest were judged on more than just beauty, though at that time it was quite acceptable to judge women on their beauty alone. The quests were very successful and ran for a number of years attracting thousands of people to the beach.

This photo also reminds me that for a few years in the 1950s we had two Sunday newspapers, *The Sunday Mail* and *The Sunday Advertiser*. *The Mail* was produced by Murdoch's News Ltd and *The Sunday Advertiser* tried to grab some of its weekend audience. The experiment was not successful and the production of *The Sunday Advertiser* ceased in December 1955.

1966

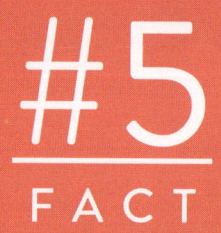

# #5
## FACT

Rundle Mall is a great place to shop, watch the passing crowd and meet up with a friend. And what better place to rendezvous than at the 'Beehive Corner', Bert Flugelman's four-metre steel balls ('The Mall's Balls') or Marguerite Derricourt's bronze pigs: Oliver, August, Horatio and Truffles?

Did you collect the Top 40 chart, compiled and printed by the local radio stations to tell you how new songs were going on the various playlists? In 1958 Radio 5AD became the first station in Adelaide to make their 'Top 40' chart available through various city and suburban record shops. 5KA soon followed, listing the 'Official Top 50' and 5DN had 'The Top 60' chart. I was an avid collector of the charts and religiously collected them from the late 1950s until I got into radio in 1965.

Here is the 5KA Top 50 from 9 September 1966 and features photos of the station announcers at that time. How many of these announcers do you remember?
ARW

# OFFICIAL 5KA TOP 50

**5KA — 5AU — 5RM**

GOOD GUY SURVEY — WEEK COMMENCING: 9th SEPTEMBER 1966

THE 5KA GOOD GUYS

1966

| # | Title | Artist | Last Week | Weeks |
|---|---|---|---|---|
| 1. | YELLOW SUBMARINE/ELEANOR RIGBY (Parlophone) | Beatles | 1 | 2 |
| 2. | FREDDIE FEELGOOD (London) | Ray Stevens | 4 | 5 |
| 3. | SUNSHINE SUPERMAN (Epic) | Donovan | 11 | 2 |
| 4. | THEY'RE COMING TO TAKE ME AWAY (CBS) | Napoleon XIV | 2 | 3 |
| 5. | EASYFEVER E.P. (Parlophone) | Easybeats | 3 | 6 |
| 6. | STEP BACK (Clarion) | Johnny Young | 7 | 2 |
| 7. | SOMEWHERE MY LOVE (CBS) | Ray Conniff Singers | 33 | 2 |
| 8. | GUANTANAMERA (Festival) | Sandpipers | 32 | 2 |
| 9. | SPRING FEVER (Atlantic) | Tony Pass | 5 | 6 |
| 10. | BUS STOP (Parlophone) | Hollies | 6 | 8 |
| 11. | BLACK IS BLACK (Decca) | Los Bravos | 9 | 5 |
| 12. | MOTHER'S LITTLE HELPER (Decca) | Rolling Stones | 8 | 3 |
| 13. | LI'L RED RIDING HOOD (MGM) | Sam the Sham | 12 | 6 |
| 14. | ONLY YOU CAN DO IT (Phono-Vox) | Francoise Hardy | 16 | 5 |
| 15. | CAN I TRUST YOU (Decca) | Bachelors | 20 | 7 |
| 16. | I COULDN'T LIVE WITHOUT YOUR LOVE (Astor) | Petula Clark | 14 | 7 |
| 17. | MAMA (Sceptre) | B. J. Thomas | 15 | 13 |
| 18. | HOUSE IN THE COUNTRY (Philips) | Pretty Things | 23 | 2 |
| 19. | WITH A GIRL LIKE YOU (Parlophone) | The Troggs | 28 | 2 |
| 20. | SUNNY AFTERNOON (Astor) | Kinks | 25 | 8 |
| 21. | I SAW HER AGAIN (RCA) | Mamas and The Papas | 24 | 3 |
| 22. | TAR AND CEMENT (Capitol) | Verdelle Smith | 10 | 10 |
| 23. | GOIN' BACK (Philips) | Dusty Springfield | 41 | 2 |
| 24. | IT'S DARK/BAD BOY (Columbia) | Twilights | 18 | 6 |
| 25. | I WANT YOU (CBS) | Bob Dylan | 21 | 5 |
| 26. | I PUT A SPELL ON YOU (Decca) | Alan Price Set | 19 | 4 |
| 27. | SUMMER IN THE CITY (Astor) | Lovin' Spoonful | 13 | 4 |
| 28. | HIDEAWAY (Philips) | Dave Dee, Dozy, Beaky | 22 | 8 |
| 29. | THERE NEVER WILL BE ANOTHER YOU (Festival) | Chris Montez | 38 | 2 |
| 30. | GET AWAY (Columbia) | George Fame | 26 | 11 |
| 31. | NEEDLE IN A HAYSTACK (Columbia) | Twilights | — | 1 |
| 32. | JUST LIKE A WOMAN (Decca) JONATHAN KING (Philips) | Manfred Mann | 50 | 2 |
| 33. | NO, NO, NO (Spin) | Tony Barber | 17 | 3 |
| 34. | LEGAL MATTER (Festival) | The Who | 35 | 4 |
| 35. | LOVE LETTERS (RCA) | Elvis Presley | 30 | 5 |
| 36. | BORN A WOMAN (ATA) JUDY STONE (MGM) | Sandy Posey | 46 | 2 |
| 37. | LANA (London) | Roy Orbison | 27 | 11 |
| 38. | TRAINS AND BOATS AND PLANES (Sceptre) | Dionne Warwick | 29 | 7 |
| 39. | LITTLE GIRL (Stateside) | Syndicate of Sound | 31 | 6 |
| 40. | HI LILI, HI LO (Decca) | Alan Price Set | 29 | 3 |
| 41. | LOVERS OF THE WORLD UNITE (Columbia) | David & Jonathan | — | 1 |
| 42. | SUMMERTIME (Chess) | Billy Stewart | 49 | 2 |
| 43. | TOO SOON TO KNOW (London) | Roy Orbison | — | 1 |
| 44. | STRANGERS IN THE NIGHT (Reprise) | Frank Sinatra | 34 | 13 |
| 45. | YOUNGER GIRL (United Artists) CRITTERS (Philips) | Hondells | 37 | 11 |
| 46. | ALFIE (Liberty) CHER (Parlophone) | Cilla Black | 40 | 2 |
| 47. | SORROW (Philips) | Merseys | 42 | 12 |
| 48. | THE END (Kommotion) | Ja-Ar | 43 | 6 |
| 49. | SWEET PEA (Ampar) | Tommy Roe | 44 | 14 |
| 50. | HE (Verve) | Righteous Brothers | 45 | 9 |

**IN THIS WEEK:**
Too Soon to Know; Lovers of the World Unite; Needle in a Haystack.

**OUT THIS WEEK:**
Wild Thing; March of the Mods; Over, Under, Sideways, Down.

---

## JIM SLADE JOINS THE 5KA GOOD GUYS!

Monday to Friday, 10.00 p.m. to 12.00 Midnight
Sunday, 12.00 noon to 6 p.m.

*No Wonder Most People Listen to 5KA — 1200!*

# 1955

When the Regent Picture Theatre opened in Rundle Street on 29 June 1928 it was described by *The Advertiser* as a 'Palace of Art'. It contained tapestries, paintings and other artworks that made 'going to the pictures as much a cultural uplifting experience as it was entertainment'.

Indeed it was a magnificent building and picture theatre and in those pre-television days, a Saturday night out at the pictures at the Regent was a very dressy affair. Ushers wore military-style uniforms, while usherettes dressed in long gowns, the mighty Wurlitzer organ played and the people came for a real night out. A wonderful icon from another era!

Organist Knight Barnett with dancers Marlene Allen, Zeta Gill and Marilyn Marker at the Regent Theatre

*Photo by News Ltd/Newspix*

Dazzleland, the amusement park at the REMM Myer Centre which opened in 1991 and folded in 1998

*Courtesy of Mary MacTavish*

1980

The Largs Pier Hotel

*Courtesy of Ken Charlton and the Department of the Environment*

When asked what is missed the most from Adelaide of yesteryear, many people nominate Dazzleland. This was the two-storey indoor amusement park occupying the top levels of the Myer Centre in Rundle Mall. It started to operate in 1991, a few years after the Myer Centre was opened in 1988, but it never really took off the way it was hoped and it was closed in 1998. The highlight was the figure 8 rollercoaster named Jazz Junction, its track running five storeys overhead. Other attractions included dodgem cars, a carousel, giant playground, musical fountain and train. As far as I am aware Level 7 of the Myer Centre remains unoccupied.

In the 1970s and 1980s the Largs Pier Hotel began to establish its reputation as an important meeting place for Aussie bands such as Jimmy Barnes with Cold Chisel, AC/DC, The Little River Band and The Angels. In fact many local bands played there during the early days of their careers. The hotel also attracted many international acts including rock great Del Shannon in the 1970s. According to legend, Bon Scott, who later became the lead singer of AC/DC, met his wife at the Largs Pier Hotel after a gig in 1971.

Her Majesty's Theatre in Grote Street. It was originally known as the Tivoli until 1962 and was saved from demolition in the late 1970s by Don Dunstan

*State Library of South Australia B15297*

The Tivoli Theatre opened in September 1913. In 1962 the Tivoli received a £300,000 remodelling and was relaunched as Her Majesty's Theatre. In the late 1970s the building was advertised for sale and, due to concern that it might be demolished, the Dunstan Government quickly stepped in and purchased the theatre, relaunching it on 10 March 1979 as The Opera Theatre.

In its 100-plus years this venue has hosted some of the biggest names in the world of showbiz, including Lauren Bacall, WC Fields, Barry Humphries and alter ego Dame Edna Everidge, Whoopi Goldberg, Spike Milligan, Rowan Atkinson, Dame Judi Dench, Ronnie Corbett and Angela Lansbury. Most have left their mark on the theatre's autograph wall.

One of Adelaide's lost theatres: The Plaza Theatre

*Photo by News Ltd/Newspix*

Situated directly behind the Adelaide Regent Theatre, the Plaza Theatre was erected out of the old Embassy Ballroom. The cinema opened in October 1955 with Katharine Hepburn and Rossano Brazzi in *Summer Madness*. Hepburn was there in person to officially open the theatre. It was the first Adelaide theatre especially built for CinemaScope presentations. The entrance was along a laneway, which ran beside the Regent Theatre. In April 1958 *Around the World in 80 Days* started its 45-week season in the new Todd-AO process.

In February 1966, the Plaza Theatre was renamed the Paris Theatre and opened with its new signage and *The Sound of Music* in the Todd-AO process. After a run of two years and three weeks, *The Sound of Music* closed in mid 1968. A few minor features ran, but after a few months the theatre closed and was completely demolished in late 1968, to allow for the completion of a shopping arcade, which also decimated her beautiful sister theatre, the Regent Theatre.

1995

5DN radio personality Jeremy Cordeaux, 1995
*Courtesy of 5DN*

Jeremy Cordeaux ran one of the most successful local radio programs from the 1970s until he retired from the air in 2004. It was a mixture of current affairs, celebrity guests, talk back, music and entertainment and rated number one many times during the mid '70s to the mid '80s.

Cordeaux has won several awards including the Walkley for journalism, Best Talk Show Host at the New York Festival Radio Awards on several occasions, has been knighted by the Order of St John for services to the Community and has been recognised with an AM by the Order of Australia Awards.

Along with his radio career, Jeremy also worked as a newsreader with Channel 10 and Channel 7. As a successful radio entrepreneur he owned the broadcasting licences of both 5AD and 5DN before selling them to ARN, their current owners.

He is currently back on air in the evening 'talk' program on 5AA.

# #6
## FACT

How many Adelaideans are there? Well, as of mid 2012 there were 1.28 million in Greater Adelaide. However, there are many Adelaideans interstate and overseas who still think of Adelaide as home or, at least, feel a connection with the city.

# 1976

Rundle Mall was officially opened by Premier Don Dunstan on 1 September 1976. Rundle Street had become extremely congested with traffic and pedestrians and it was decided to turn the western end of the strip, from Pulteney Street to King William Street, into a pedestrian mall. In front of a huge crowd and with champagne flowing from the fountain, Mr Dunstan declared Rundle Mall open for business. There have been several major upgrades since that first opening and there is always much debate around the mall and how people feel about it. The last upgrade got a big 'thumbs down' from many commentators, but the mall remains the heart of Adelaide's retail shopping.

Rundle Mall opens in 1976. Adelaide was pretty excited at the time and champagne flowed from the fountain to celebrate the occasion

*Photo by News Ltd/Newspix*

1970

Members of the TV cast of *Number 96* in town in the 1970s for the *Channel 10 Christmas Appeal*. Some of the faces include Noel O'Connor, local TV presenter along with Debbie Byrne, Joe Hasham, Bunny Brooke, Chantal Contouri, Joe Martin, Sally Boyden, Peta Peters (Ch 10 weather girl), Pat McDonald, Jane Reilly (Ch 10 news), and Johnny Pace

*Courtesy of Noel O'Connor*

All three Adelaide commercial TV stations had an annual fund-raising event for charity. Channel 7 had *The Good Friday Appeal* for the Crippled Children Association. Channel 9 ran *Telethon*, raising money for 'The House of Hope' and Channel 10 ran its *Christmas Appeal* with stars from the network flying into Adelaide for the weekend live broadcast from SAS10 studios in Gilberton. Game show host Gary Meadows was the anchor for most years.

This is where the tune 'Thank You Very Much for Your Kind Donation' originated. It would be played whenever a major donation was announced during the broadcast with members of the cast forming a conga line and dancing around the studio.

## 1960

It's over 50 years since the Savoy Theatre closed. It reopened shortly after as the Globe Theatrette, which only operated for 18 months.

The Savoy showed the latest newsreels from Cinesound Review or Movietone News. I recall it was 1/- for a child's ticket and the sessions would run for about an hour. The newsreel theatrettes started during the war years, when people were anxious to find out the latest developments from the front, and lasted until the early 1960s, by which time TV had come along and taken away their audience. You'd get the latest news and generally a comedy short like a *Steve Smith Special*, and possibly a cartoon.

Great photo of the Savoy, possibly in 1960 not long before it became the Globe

*Frank Hall Courtesy of Elaine Hall*

# 1953

The Redex Trials became all the rage in the mid-century and remained very popular until well into the 1960s. I remember all the publicity the drivers got with regular and dramatic reports on the wireless about the tough conditions the drivers had to endure as they drove through the outback of Australia and how 'Gelignite Jack', one of the more notorious drivers, would light a stick of gelignite and try to blow up competitors' cars. The rallies, especially in the early years were tremendously popular as the roads linking large portions of the country, particularly west of Adelaide, were not in good condition. Car manufacturers were enthusiastic about the event as it provided a good test for their products, proving their cars were able to stand up to remote Australian conditions. I remember it was the first time I heard of a car called a 'Volkswagen', which won five of the first nine Redex and Ampol Trials run between 1953 and 1958.

Redex Trial competitors at Norwood Oval
Photo by News Ltd/Newspix

1953

1959

# #7
## FACT

Light's Vision on Montefiore Hill, North Adelaide, is a statue commemorating Adelaide's first surveyor-general, Colonel William Light: the man who famously devised the city plan with its squares, surrounding Parklands and memorable grid pattern.

# 1959

A TAA Fokker Friendship coming into land at what was Adelaide's main airport until 1954. Parafield Airport was first developed in 1927 but by 1947, the demand on aviation had outgrown it and the current site of Adelaide Airport was selected at West Torrens (now West Beach). Construction began and flights commenced to and from there in 1954. Looking up King's Road, the rolling hillside in the background is now the suburb of Para Hills.

*Advertiser* photographer Pat Crowe captured this amazing photo of the Fokker Friendship, *Abel Tasman*, arriving at Parafield Airport in 1959. The very same plane crashed in Queensland in June 1960 killing all on board (29 people) in Australia's worst aviation disaster

Photo by Pat Crowe/Newspix

1959

The Royal Adelaide Show is the annual agricultural show and fair that begins on the first Friday in September, and runs for nine days. It is held at the Adelaide Showgrounds in Wayville and is attended by thousands. It features food, rides, a ferris wheel, competitions and animal races.

'The Show' is primarily an opportunity for the State's farmers to show examples of their livestock. There is also horticulture on display with fresh fruit and vegetables. There's a cakes and scones competition, jams and pickles on display and prizes for millinery.

1959

Mum and Dad with the kids at the annual treat, a day at The Show in 1959. After months of saving up, all the show bags on offer will be inspected and one or two carefully chosen

*Photo by News Ltd/Newspix*

61

## 1968

The ABC commenced broadcasting as 5CL in the 1930s (later 5AN) out of two buildings in Hindmarsh Square. One of the buildings had been used as horse stables, the other as a Congregational church. Referred to by staff as a 'rabbit warren' of offices, they were not sound-proof, so if someone spoke too loudly in the nearby foyer the noise would be picked up by the studio microphone. In 1959, the ABC bought Tregenna, an old mansion in Collinswood on a four-and-a-half acre block, and it was set up as offices for television staff. In the early 1970s Tregenna was demolished, making way for an eight-storey building where the rest of the ABC staff relocated in 1974.

The old ABC buildings in the Square were demolished in the early 1980s in the middle of the night by the Adelaide City Council, to avoid any protests like those associated with the Aurora Hotel demolition.

The old ABC Building on the eastern side of Hindmarsh Square, with the Aurora Hotel in the distance
*Frank Hall, courtesy of Elaine Hall*

Sir Thomas Playford Premier of South Australia from 1938 to 1965
*Wikipedia*

No other Australian leader, state or federal, has served longer than Sir Thomas Playford, who spent 26 years as Premier of South Australia. It was a time of enormous change for Adelaide and the State. Playford was the driving force behind the creation of the Electricity Trust of SA, he steered the construction of the Mannum to Adelaide pipeline, guided the expansion of the Housing Trust and oversaw the development of the suburb of Elizabeth. He brought industries such as Philips and Uniroyal to South Australia, convinced Holden and Chrysler to expand their manufacturing operations in South Australia, and brought the defence industry here as well.

In the year before he took office South Australia, had a population of around 591,000 and when he left it was over 1 million people.

## 1954

Schooldays: playing outside on the swings, slippery dips, see-saws and other equipment that, from memory, seemed to have very little thought put into the safety aspect. I can recall (you probably can too) hanging upside down from the monkey bars, climbing to the top of the climbing bars, jumping off the hurdy-gurdy, swinging as hard as you could on a swing and jumping off at full height because somebody 'double-dared' you.

I came off the monkey bars once and landed on the back of my head, came off my bike a dozen times and landed once on my face. I recall a school friend of mine breaking his arm in the playground, but by and large most of us got through without too much damage.

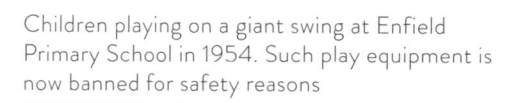

Children playing on a giant swing at Enfield Primary School in 1954. Such play equipment is now banned for safety reasons

*Photo by News Ltd/Newspix*

1954

## 1989

Did you save addresses and telephone numbers in a 'Teledex'?

I know it seems silly, but I still have a Teledex in my office drawer which has telephone numbers and addresses that I wrote in it back in the '80s sometime.

Teledexes were so simple, put the little indicator on the letter, press the button on the bottom and, there you are, the address and phone number of the person you were looking for ... almost as easy as looking it up on your iPhone! LOL.

Have you kept your old Teledex?

Intense concentration shows on the face of Adelaide tennis great Mark Woodforde as he delivers a double backhander in the final of the SA Open at Memorial Drive in 1989

*Photo by Paul Lakatos/Newspix*

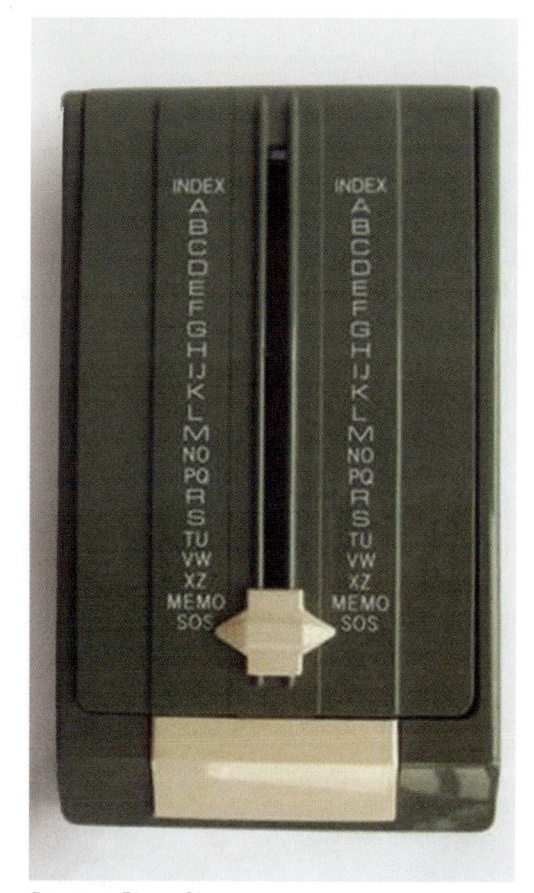

The Adelaide International tournament was played at Memorial Drive from 1974 until 2007.

Since its inception in 1921 Memorial Drive has featured on the world stage of tennis with many major events held on the grass courts including the Davis Cup and Australian Open Championships. In 1958 Pancho Gonzalez and Lew Hoad appeared at Memorial Drive as part of Jack Kramer's professional troupe.

Sadly, it's estimated about $20million is needed to return Memorial Drive to world standards. Many people hoped it might be part of the Adelaide Oval upgrade, but it was not to be, so we live in hope that international competition will one day return to Memorial Drive.

*Pinterest Photo Sharing*

1947

Ugh. I was a shocker when it came to playing sport (got my first pair of glasses aged 9). I just never seemed to get the hang of it. But every year I'd have to join in with all the other kids and run and jump, grab the baton and run like hell, fall flat on my face in the sack race, and watch the other kids get the trophies at the end of the day.

This photo was taken in 1947 at the Adelaide Oval during a school sports day. Wonder if they'll still be able to hold a school sports day at the new stadium?

Remember your school sports day?

*Photo by News Ltd/Newspix*

### 1972

One of Adelaide's all-time favourite bands was Cold Chisel. They originally started in about 1974 as a heavy-metal cover band and are recognised today along with another Adelaide group The Angels, as among the pioneers of pub rock in Australia.

Pub Rock is unique to this country and was mainly popular in the 1970s and 1980s. Most of the venues were hot and crowded inner-city or suburban pubs and the crowds were in their late teens or early twenties. Pubs that quickly come to mind are the Largs Pier, Governor Hindmarsh and Pooraka Hotels, but there were plenty more and I'm sure many people will remember their own favourite pub.

Australian musicologist Ian McFarlane describes Cold Chisel's music on Wikipedia as:

1972

Singer Jimmy Barnes pulled from crowd during one of Cold Chisel band's concerts in 1970s

*Photo by News Ltd/Newspix*

a combination of rockabilly, hard rock and rough-house soul'n'blues that was defiantly Australian in outlook. [He notes that The Angels had] a profound effect on the Australian live music scene of the late 1970s and early '80s. They helped redefine the Australian pub rock tradition, their brand of no-frills, hard-driving boogie rock attracted pub-goers in unprecedented numbers.

# 1989

*Glen Dix, with his flamboyant flag-waving style, brings home the winner of the 1989 Adelaide Grand Prix*

Photo by News Ltd/Newspix

Did you ever go to an Adelaide Grand Prix and see Glen Dix, one of the state's most famous racing identities, waving the black and white flag?

Glen has been involved in motorsport in South Australia since the mid 1950s. He started out Speedway racing and by the time of the first Adelaide Grand Prix in 1985 he had been waving the chequered flag for some 30 years, at Rowley Park Speedway and at Malalla.

Glen's flamboyant flag-waving style was famous all over the world. So too was his favourite golden jacket, something that he was responsible for introducing: 'The golden jacket was my own idea, when I knew I was going to wave the chequered flag, I asked if I could dress myself in the national colours, the green and gold.'

# #8
## FACT

Adelaide Casino is the only licensed casino in the state. Housed in the Adelaide Railway Station on North Terrace it opened in 1985 and employs over a thousand people.

## 1979

The year was 1979 and sure we had the latest in electronic gadgetry with transistor radios, tape decks and the like and then Sony introduced something that would play your latest cassette while you were out jogging or walking. In that first year alone the Sony Walkman sold millions around the world and, believe it or not, mine still works today.

I was off to the footy last year and the batteries in my very small compact radio had died and I was searching around for a radio to take with me. I had a couple of AA batteries that fitted my son's old Walkman, so I took it with me to the footy. My son couldn't believe his eyes when he saw his beloved old Walkman still working, and my 21-year-old nephew, having never seen a Sony Walkman before, had to have it explained to him!

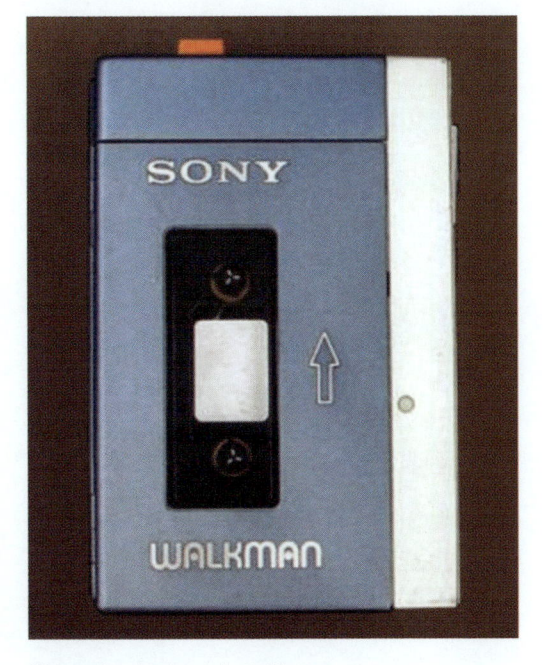

*Wikipedia, Author joho345*

## 1981

Max Fatchen was the Adelaide columnist with the longest output, producing columns in *The News* from 1948 and *The Advertiser* from 1955 to way past his retirement in 1984, in fact until his last piece that was printed just a few days before his death age 92 in 2012.

After his retirement, his career as a children's book writer blossomed. His book, *The River Kings*, was published in six countries and four languages and the ensuing television series was screened in more than 40 countries.

Max Fatchen, 1981. South Australia's most-loved wordsmith: columnist, journalist, novelist and poet

*Photo by News Ltd/Newspix*

King William Street with the old Advertiser Building, on the right, taken from the top of the T&G Building in the 1950s

*Frank Hall, courtesy of Elaine Hall*

1950

This was when King William Street ran through the centre of Victoria Square. To the right of the square the Moore's sign (Charles Moores Department Store) can clearly be seen. There's also the back of the old toilet block in the square itself and the old Criterion Hotel (with the Orlando sign), then the 5AD building and behind that the old Advertiser building. At the back is the building that housed the printing presses for the paper and Advertiser Lane where you would dash every year to get exam results as soon as they came off the press!

Across Waymouth Street all those little buildings have all been replaced ... In fact, most of these buildings have now gone. Town Hall and the Post Office are the same. Notice the angle parking along King William Street.

# 1957

Debutante Balls were a very important annual event on the social calendar in any suburb or town throughout the 1950s and 1960s. It was a coming-of-age tradition where young women were introduced to society, originally indicating the girls had reached an age where they were eligible for marriage. The girls would invite a young beau to be their escort for the evening and after dinner the debutantes were presented to a leading dignitary. Finally, the evening wound up with some ballroom dancing.

A weird craze took off in the 1950s and made a bit of a comeback in the late 1970s. It involved sitting on top of a pole for as long as possible in a bid to win a prize or to raise money for a charity. The participants would use a system of buckets and pulleys to transport food, drinks and donations from onlookers on the ground below. Temperatures on the day this photo was taken apparently reached 110 degrees Fahrenheit (43 degrees Celsius), but the pole-sitters stuck it out, despite the high temperatures. I bet they wouldn't have minded one of those ice-creams advertised in the lower right-hand corner!

These young ladies and their partners were making their debut at Payneham in 1957

*Photo by News Ltd/Newspix*

1959

Four of the six pole-sitters who sat atop a pole for up to three days at Henley Beach carnival in 1959

*Photo by News Ltd/Newspix*

1960

Did your neighbours used to come together on 5 November for Guy Fawkes' night? We would bring whatever we wanted to burn, make a straw Guy and dress him in old pants and a coat and sit him atop the pile. When the sun went down the bonfire would be lit and there would be penny bombs exploding, Catherine wheels whizzing and sky rockets flying into the air. It was always well supervised with the adults usually lighting most of the crackers.

We got special money to buy our favourites for the event and, of course, had to write our names with sparklers when we were smaller. The following day everybody was up early to see if they could find any un-exploded fireworks, which prompted a repeat performance, but this time without the bonfire.

Guy Fawkes Night was a special event in the neighbourhood when all the families got together for a big bonfire

Photo by News Ltd/Newspix

# #9
## FACT

The Ash Wednesday bushfire was a disastrous day in South Australian and Victorian history. On 16 February 1983, 28 South Australians died and 47 people in Victoria. The Adelaide Hills were hard-hit, with some 50 houses destroyed by fire.

1946

Preparing a camp breakfast at the Oakbank Picnic Races, Easter 1946

*Photo by News Ltd/Newspix*

For decades, many Adelaide families have made the annual trek to Oakbank for the picnic race meeting there every Easter and to camp in the grounds for a full week or more.

Oakbank is the biggest Picnic Race meeting on earth attracting crowds up to 70,000 people. For many South Australian children it is the amusements and kids activities such as show rides, sideshows, kiddies zoo, face painting and other entertainment – and of course there's always the horse racing.

## 1949

Most boomer kids' mothers sewed: either making clothes for the children or mending rips and tears from vigorous games and what would be considered dangerous activities today. My mother had been a tailoress (something she was extremely proud of) before her marriage and was a dab hand with the Singer pedal sewing machine.

She made frocks for my sisters and school clothes for me. I suspect most mums back then accepted it as part of their role of cooking, cleaning, making beds and scrubbing floors, darning socks and keeping the home fires burning.

A very early Singer Treadle Sewing Machine

*Wikipedia, photo Thomas Gozdziewicz*

For many years the West End Brewery was situated in Hindley Street in Adelaide and, although it's not clearly visible in this photo, had a very tall chimney that became a cultural landmark. Each year the colours of the premier SANFL football team were painted on the chimney and remained there for 12 months.

The West End brewery was operational from the late 1800s to 1980 when the

1970

The West End Brewery in Hindley Street, prior to its closure in 1980

State Library of South Australia B42331

One of South Australia's most colourful winemakers, Wolf Blass

Photo by News Ltd/Newspix

company moved operations to the Southwark plant on Port Road and the building was demolished in 1982. It was the last brewery remaining in the City of Adelaide, having outlasted fifteen others. The reason given for its closure was that it had outgrown the facilities on Hindley Street. The tradition of painting the footy premier's colours was moved to Thebarton.

The South Australian wine industry has produced some great personalities over the years, among them Wolf Blass. Wolf, left Germany and came to Australia in 1961 with his winemaking diploma and very little else. He started out as a winemaker with TST (Tolley, Scott and Tolley), but before long began to produce his own brand with a unique style and character. He produced both red and white styles and at one stage reportedly claimed that his wines 'would make strong women weak and weak men strong'!

Wolf was a showman and a very clever marketer and it wasn't long before his wine began to win a swag of awards. He was also an excellent winemaker and continued to create new and interesting styles until he finally sold Wolf Blass Wines to Mildura Wines in the early '90s.

# 1924

The Grand Central Hotel stood on the corner of Rundle and Pulteney Streets. This magnificent building was erected in 1911, and was so grand and imposing it could be seen from anywhere along the length of Rundle Street. 'The Grand' unfortunately did not prosper, despite having many important guests, including the Prince of Wales during his visit to Adelaide in 1920.

The Grand was eventually sold to Foy & Gibson in 1924 (probably around the time this photo was taken), who established a department store in the building and continued to use it until the mid 1950s. Foy & Gibson then left the old building to take over newly built premises in Rundle Street, there trading as Cox Foys.

The Government then acquired it to house the administration of several departments. Although strictly an Edwardian building, it was the only example of high Victorian-style architecture that Adelaide possessed. Sadly, the building was demolished in the mid 1970s to make way for a multistorey car park and a Hungry Jacks, which is still there today.

The Grand Central Hotel, 1924
State Library of South Australia B72783/3

1970

In the early 1970s the building that originally started out as the Grand Central Hotel housed several State Government Departments, including ETSA

*Frank Hall, courtesy of Elaine Hall*

Here we see the striking facade of what had been the Grand Central Hotel, then a department store and finally the offices of State Government public service departments, including ETSA (owned by the government before being sold off in bits and privatised).

Apparently the Government of the day allowed the property to eventually become very rundown before deciding to demolish it.

'This deserted playground took me back to the playgrounds of my youth, full of what would now be considered dangerous equipment'

Courtesy of Andrew Heslop

Andrew Heslop, Social Entrepreneur, Commentator and Community Advocate, is a regular contributor to our Facebook page and recently posted the photo of the deserted playground with this explanation:

Driving inland between Adelaide and Canberra a few weeks ago I came across this deserted playground at a tiny place called Eurongilly. The equipment is what caught my eye and if you look closely between the slippery dip and the hurdy-gurdy you'll see a jungle gym.

It doesn't look as though kids have played here for a long time – and I sure scared the daylights out of a kangaroo that had been resting in the shade. But once parks across Adelaide were filled with such dangerous equipment and I had many happy days on the Semaphore foreshore as my mum and grandmother were instructed to push the hurdy-gurdy faster and faster! Of course they warned me about falling off and even jumping off at a slow speed (on to the lawn) reminding me how easy it was to get hurt. So I learned not to do it.

1964

# #10
## FACT

In February 1964 'The Blair Schwartz Show' on Channel 7, was telecast for the first time. Blair was a wonderfully talented entertainer and media personality in Adelaide during the 1950s and 1960s and was breakfast announcer on Radio 5AD before he left to join Channel 7 as part of its opening line-up in 1959. He was involved in many of those early live shows on local TV. Many people also remember him for his live appearances around Adelaide and as a regular member of the group who played at the Pizza Palace on Anzac Highway in the 1960s.

It's a shame that TV is no longer local and everything now comes 'canned' from Melbourne and Sydney. Sure, they're big, sophisticated productions, beautifully produced and professionally executed, and if we looked back at some of our local TV shows they could appear amateurish and probably even embarrassing. But, they were local and fun and we had local personalities with the opportunity to display local talent. We lived through an amazing era of local TV in Adelaide from the late 1950s to the 1980s.

The much-loved 'Popeye' boats are privately owned ferries that operate between Elder Park and the Adelaide Zoo. The first boat was launched on the Torrens Lake by Gordon Watts in 1935 and they are now well and truly part of Adelaide's treasured heritage.

Local TV personality and a great entertainer, Blair Schwartz

*State Library of South Australia B70869/17701*

## 1967

Adelaide's own Bev Harrell became a national pop star back in the 1960s. Bev started her singing career at the age of 6 when she first appeared on 5AD's *Kangaroos on Parade* and in 1967 won Best Female Vocal in the 5KA Top Talent Award. Her first recording that year, 'What Am I Doing Here With You?', was an instant hit and reached Number One not only in Adelaide, but also nationally. Bev did most of the dances around town and became a real crowd favourite and also travelled to South Australian country areas where she performed in Town Halls and Institutes. She followed up her big hit with two more chart successes that same year. Bev still lives in Adelaide and still performs both locally and nationally.

The old Gresham Hotel being demolished in 1965
*State Library of South Australia B16198*

Petite (4'9") blonde pop vocalist Bev Harrell one of the most popular female solo singers in Adelaide and also Australia in the late 1960s

*ACA Entertainment*

1965

Adelaide was once called 'The City of Churches', but it could just as easily have been 'The City of Pubs'. This was not an image that the colonial fathers encouraged, even though at one time there were twice as many pubs in the Adelaide square mile as churches.

The Gresham Hotel had the enviable address of number 1 King William Street, on the southwest corner of North Terrace and King William Street, one of Adelaide's most prominent commercial sites. Built in 1873–74, it was described as a plain building with a large cast-iron veranda and balcony. It was replaced by a huge glass tower that for many years was the headquarters of AMP, but is now the city branch of Westpac Bank.

## 1963

Adelaide was known for the production of Holdens at Woodville and Elizabeth, and of the Chrysler range at Tonsley Park. But did you know we also produced the Zeta in Camden Park? The Zeta was manufactured by Lightburn & Co from 1963 to 1965. Lightburn made cement mixers and washing machines in its factory and I believe the Zeta had the cement-mixer motor. The first Zeta model was introduced in 1963 at a price of £595. From memory it had three forward gears and no reverse! Production ceased in 1965, with the last vehicles sold in 1966 and total sales of fewer than 400 vehicles.

1963

Adelaide was home to the production of several motor cars. Remember the Lightburn Zeta? This was the 'sports' sedan with models Ann Francis and Prue Holmes

*Photo by News Ltd/Newspix*

# #11
## FACT

Robyn Archer is a well-loved singer, cabaret artist, yodeller and festival director here and abroad. Born and educated in Adelaide, her musical talents have taken her far afield as both performer and artistic director.

# 1959

They were called the Courtesy Patrol, however as a young teenager I don't recall much of the courtesy. The police had a different attitude in those days. If you mucked up, you were more likely to get a clip around the ear and told to behave yourself or next time you'd be in trouble. You would not dare go home and tell your parents a cop had twisted your ear because then you'd be in even bigger trouble with your parents for getting in trouble with the police!

Kenny Peplow's family heads off for the Easter break, 1960s

*Courtesy of Kenny Peplow*

The SA Police Courtesy Patrol in 1959

*State Library of South Australia BRG 347/1267 Courtesy of the Arthur Family Photographic Collection*

1958

At Easter many Adelaideans would head off to the Flinders or up the Murray River, over to Yorke Peninsula or down to Victor Harbor. Caravans were pretty basic during my childhood: no seat belts, no air-conditioning and no digital games to keep kids quiet.

A butcher at the Adelaide Central Market calls out his reduced meat prices to shoppers in an effort to get their custom, 1958

*Photo by News Ltd/Newspix*

The Adelaide Central Market has been in existence for more than 100 years and is now regarded as an icon of the city and something that every visitor should experience. Over the years the market has gone through both difficult and thriving times but has always remained a true part of Adelaide's character.

On Fridays during the 1950s, more than 5000 people would jostle for bargains in the Meat Hall. Competing butchers would reduce meat to 'giveaway' prices in what became a Friday lunch time attraction for housewives and city workers.

**1960**

If you were lucky enough to get to Victor Harbor for the school holidays, one of the highlights was a ride on the chairlift to Granite Island.

Lindsay Honeyman, driver of the horse-drawn tram from Victor to the Island for 13 years recalled some of the attractions on Granite Island in a recent media release:

> There was the chairlift in the 1960s. There was also a strange cage that was hoisted up a 40-foot pylon and dropped – it was called a Space Steeple, a sort of early thrill ride.
>
> And for a while, there were wallabies here, but they denuded the place and had to go. The biggest events were always the New Year's Day celebrations held on the island. There'd be 30,000 people, all swimming, picnicking and partying.

## 1948

The Granite Island chairlift: installed in 1964 and removed in 1996
*Alex Prichard/Flickr*

A 'servo' belonging to Michael Brodie's grandfather on Fullarton Road and Ferguson Avenue shortly after World War II
Courtesy of Michael Brodie

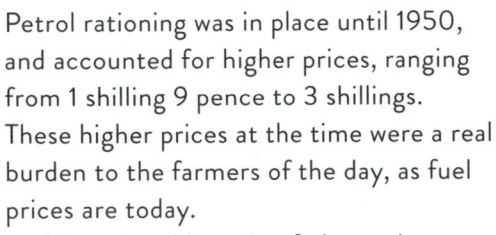

Petrol rationing was in place until 1950, and accounted for higher prices, ranging from 1 shilling 9 pence to 3 shillings. These higher prices at the time were a real burden to the farmers of the day, as fuel prices are today.

Note the old gravity-fed petrol pumps and also the outside hoist.

The Victor Harbor dodgem cars were another holiday attraction in the 1960s
Courtesy of Di Quick

91

1 9 5 0

# 1950

Stephen Bradshaw shared some memories about growing up in Adelaide in the 1950s and '60s:

> I grew up in Adelaide, went to the City Baths a lot. Lockers were 6d and you would fix the key on your bathers with a hair pin. A good treat was having a bush biscuit, lying up on the 3-metre area on your towel, and you could get a shot of brylcream to do your hair after swimming for about 3d.

The City Baths were a big feature if you grew up in Adelaide and couldn't get to the beach. The Baths, where the Festival Centre is now, were a hive of activity every summer before swimming pools became more easily available for suburban backyards. They were completely demolished in 1969.

A hive of activity at the City Baths on a hot Adelaide summer's day in the 1950s

*Photo by Bill Krischock/Newspix*

1979

Moores on the Square, now known as the Sir Samuel Way Building. You can still get a sense of the magnificence of the original building

*State Library of South Australia B69526*
*Photograph by Jenny Scott*

# 1979

On 27 December 1979, 'Moore's on the Square', which had been a shopping institution in Adelaide for more than 50 years, closed its doors for the final time! Moore's had opened their 'new palatial store on the west side of Victoria Square between Gouger and Grote Streets' in 1916. No expense was spared in providing a maximum of display area behind large plate-glass windows, generously lit by a huge leadlight cupola and extensive artificial lighting. A feature was the grand marble staircase leading to the first floor.

On 2 March 1948 Moore's was gutted by fire (one of Adelaide's biggest ever) and all that remained was some ground-floor structures, the external shell, and that magnificent staircase. The shop was completely rebuilt and business returned, until its gradual decline in the 1970s. In 1979 the store was sold to the South Australian Government and was later transformed into the major law courts.

## 1986

Adelaide's basketball team the Adelaide 36ers reached new heights under Ken Cole in the mid 1980s at Apollo Stadium. Ken had been a champion player of the game before taking on the coaching role. Suddenly Adelaide was enjoying a golden era of success in the game. Cole was a flamboyant and controversial character who dressed impeccably and exercised great control over his talented players. After a highly successful season in 1985, Cole went on to produce 'The Invincibles' of '86, who lost just two games in the entire season.

The inimitable coach of the Adelaide 36ers, Ken Cole, who took basketball to a new level in the mid 1980s with 'The Invincibles'

*Photo by News Ltd/Newspix*

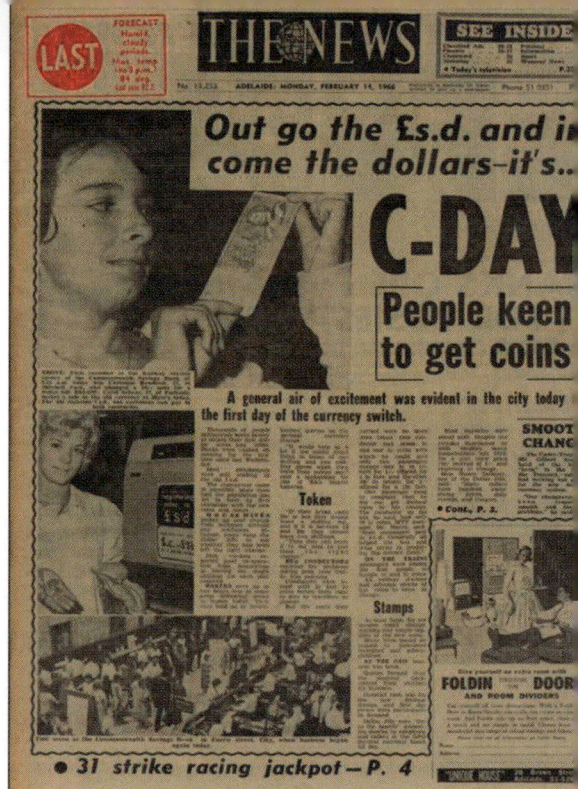

'In come the dollars, in come the cents.' People travelled to the city especially for the day to get some of the new money

*State Library of South Australia*

Decimal currency was first introduced into Australia on 14 February 1966. 'C-day' was for 'conversion' or 'changeover' day. We had a jingle which we played on the radio and there was also a TV commercial made and sung to the tune of 'Click Go the Shears', to signal the changeover from pounds, shillings and pence to dollars and cents. *The News* of 14 February 1966 reported that: 'A general air of excitement was evident in the city today for the first day of currency switch. Thousands of people deliberately spent money to obtain their first dollar notes and coins.'

# 1970

The Adelaide Fruit and Produce Exchange or the East End Market opened on 2 May 1904. Various extensions ensued over the next few years, and by 1910, there were 390 growers' stands (with provision for their vehicles and teams), 20 large packing stores, 11 small stores, 10 side stores, a refreshment room and a blacksmith.

Nearly four acres were developed for market purposes and it was once described as 'the best of its character in Australia – lofty, well-ventilated, wide roads, no obstacles, automatically drained, and kept wonderfully clean.'

The markets traded successfully up until the late 1980s at which time they were relocated out of the City to the northern suburb of Pooraka. The site of the old market was redeveloped as apartment buildings, maintaining most of the old buildings and its original character.

*I always loved the comings and goings of the East End Market on East Terrace. Trucks parked in the middle of the road and fresh produce was everywhere. Always had great energy!*

*Photo by News Ltd/Newspix*

1954

Ballroom dancing at the Palais Royale in North Terrace in the 1950s
Photo by News Ltd/Newspix

The Palais Royale was a dance and entertainment centre for more than 50 years. It opened in 1920 and continued as a main venue for everything from concerts to ballroom dancing. There were lots of dances there for the youngsters of the late 1950s and early 1960s.

It was gradually replaced by newer, more modern venues and, in 1967, was turned into a parking station before being completely demolished in 1972 and replaced with an apartment building.

Do you remember going to dances at the Palais?

1960

Radiograms were most popular in the post-war era and suddenly mushroomed in sales when 45s and 33s came onto the market in the mid to late 1950s. One of the main features of the radiogram was the record autochanger, which would accept up to 10 records and play them one after another. Such technology!

I recall that some of the singles would feature a 'non-slip' label, very important to have a non-slip label between the labels that had no grip, otherwise the record would slip and not play properly.

Radiograms started to disappear in the late 1960s after the development of the transistor when smaller more portable record players were developed. Philips Industries made radiograms here in Adelaide at their Hendon Plant.

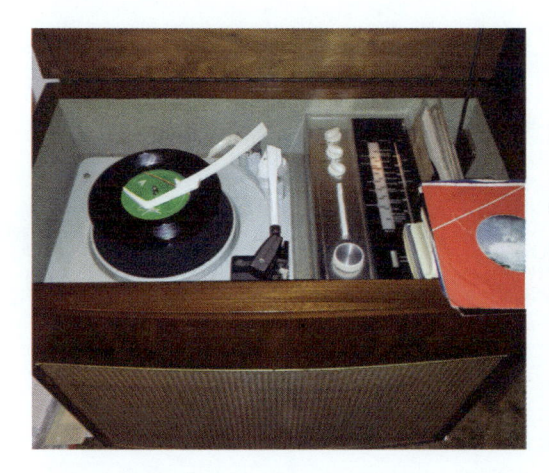

Here's a radiogram from the 1960s that's still going strong today, complete with the 45s on the record changer

*Courtesy of Dale Sanders*

# #12
FACT

The University Footbridge spans the Torrens River, connecting the back of the University of Adelaide with North Adelaide. In 1972 lecturer Dr George Duncan was drowned there. As a direct consequence, in 1975 South Australian law was reformed and the state was the first to decriminalise homosexuality.

# 1976

The biggest crowd ever at an SANFL footy grand final was at Footy Park in 1976 when about 76,000 fans packed into the grounds for the game between Sturt and Port Adelaide. The crowd was officially estimated at 66,697, but it was later revealed that even greater numbers had been allowed to enter the ground. Eventually officials realised the potential for a disaster and allowed part of the huge crowd onto the perimeter of the oval inside the fence to watch the game. Some fans later complained that it was not the ideal spot from which to watch the game, but there's no denying they were close to the action that day. Sturt won the game by 41 points.

There wasn't even standing room at the 1976 Grand Final between Sturt and Port Adelaide at Footy Park. Some members of the crowd were advised to sit on the inside of the oval fence to ease the crowd congestion

*Photo by News Ltd/Newspix*

1954

Bathing beauties line up at Semaphore beach in 1954 hoping to win the title!

*Photo by News Ltd/Newspix*

Bathing beauty contests were popular events during the 1950s to the 1970s. It was not unusual for thousands of people to turn up on the beach to watch a local bathing beauty competition conducted with both heats and a final.

Prizes were often large sums of money and included a trip interstate for a crack at the national title. Some young women went on to create a career in the media or similar professions after winning a beauty contest. Adelaide's own Jane Reilly won the national title in 1974 and went on to become a weather presenter and children's program host on local television and is still involved in media today.

1 9 6 3

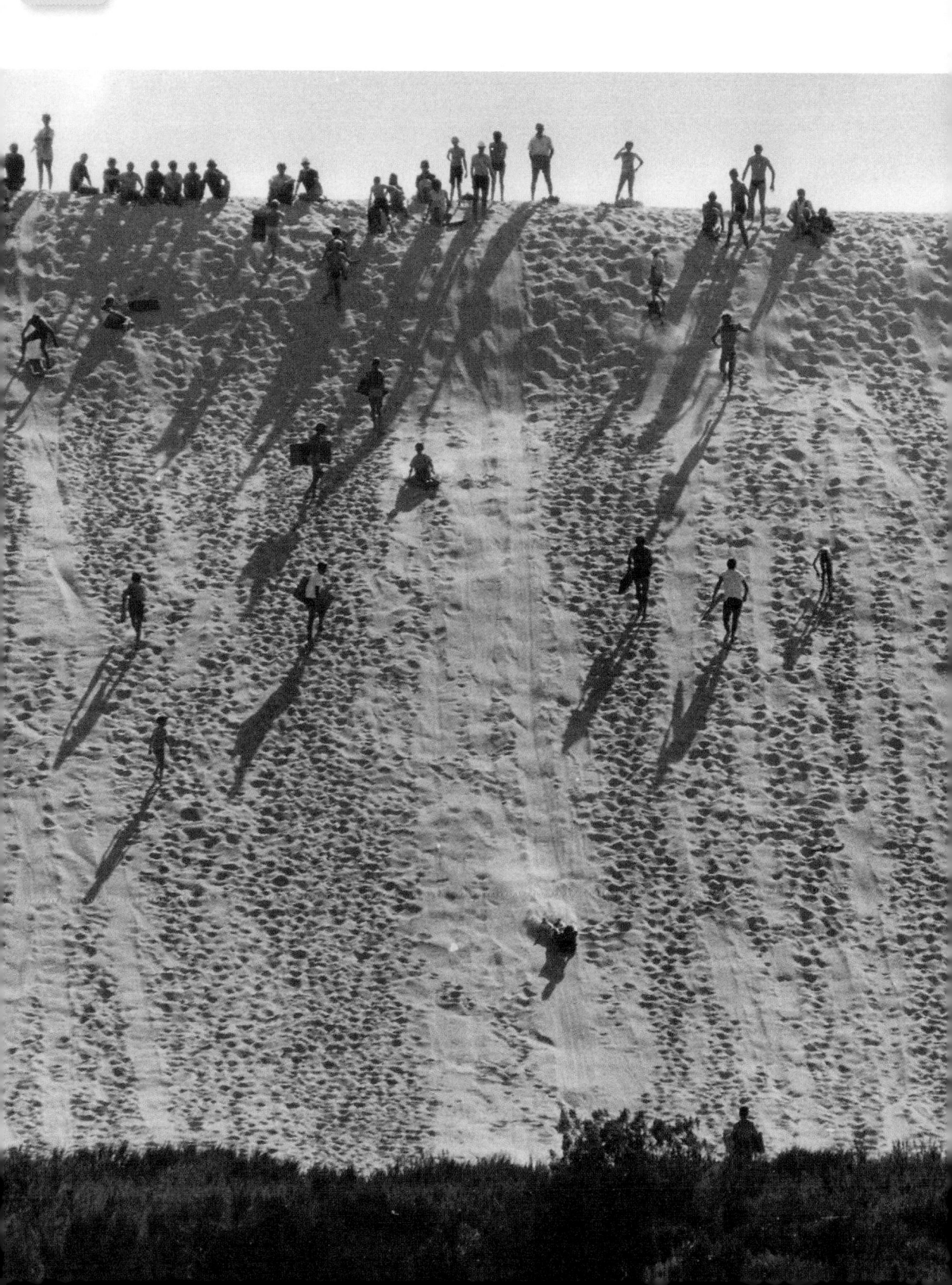

## 1963

Kids growing up in Adelaide could go to the beach all day during school holidays. You'd ride your bike there in the morning, leave it without a padlock (never owned one), play at the beach, slide down the massive sandhills at Port Noarlunga or swim and dive off the jetty, grab a Chiko roll or pastie for lunch (or a bush biscuit with butter and Vegemite), and your parents wouldn't worry about where you were or if you were getting up to mischief. Parents were a lot less protective and everything was a lot cheaper. If you didn't have any money, just find a few empty Coke bottles or a Woodies soft drink bottle (6d return for the large bottle), cash it in and you'd have enough to feed yourself. It was simple, uncomplicated fun and by the time you got home (before the street lights went on) you would be totally exhausted and sunburned, but ready to do it all again the next day.

Sliding down the huge sandhills at Port Noarlunga, 1960s

*Photo by News Ltd/Newspix*

## 1995

The public lawns and bandstand at Glenelg pictured here in 1995 have long been popular cooling-off spots on hot summer nights

*Courtesy of Ken Taylor*

Before air-conditioners and fans there was the beach or a fresh evening breeze on the front veranda. Dad would hose the outside walls of the house once the blazing hot sun went down and then we'd take the wireless out with us to listen to our favourite radio serials. The neighbours would be doing the same thing and some would wander past and say 'Good evening' and stop for a brief chat about how hot it was. If Mum found a couple of shillings, one of us would be allowed to walk down to the corner shop or deli to buy a cold bottle of Woodies Lemonade as a treat for the night. If it hadn't cooled down by bedtime, we were allowed to sleep out on the lawn until the mozzies would drive you inside to your bed at about 1am.

Some families would stay at the beach and head home only once it cooled down enough to be able to sleep inside.

## 1996

The old News building in North Terrace had been deserted for a number of years and was due for demolition when it caught fire in 1996. Reportedly squatters camped in the building started the blaze.

*The News* had a long history in Adelaide, starting out as the *Evening Journal* in 1869 and was bought from *The Herald and Weekly Times* in 1949 by Sir Keith Murdoch. It was the main asset passed to his son Rupert upon his death. It was Rupert's first media interest and set the foundation of what was to become News Limited and subsequently the international media conglomerate, News Corporation.

Later Murdoch acquired the other local paper, *The Advertiser* in 1987. Rupert Murdoch sold *The News* that year and many of its journalists moved to *The Advertiser*. *The News* closed in 1992.

The Sebel Playford Hotel now stands on the site.

A spectacular blaze devours the old News building in 1996

*Photo by News Ltd/Newspix*

## 1951

A year or so ago the ABC TV show *Who's Been Sleeping in My House* told a story relating to an Adelaide house with a mysterious past. The house was supposed to be the location of a radio station shut down during World War II for sending radio messages to German warships about the movement of troopships leaving Australia for the war. They carried on about a secret transmitter in the roof etc., but never got near the real truth. I worked for the 5KA network for five years and this is my understanding of what happened.

Early in 1940, due to the war, broadcasting regulations were altered and all broadcasts were censored, with weather reports banned totally. The government was also concerned about pacifists. 5KA was owned by the Jehovah Witness Church and they were opposed to war.

In 1941, the Naval Department closed 5KA. The reason given, but not made public, was that Victoria Reynolds, Social Editor of *The Advertiser*, had allegedly said on air: 'As I was coming to work today, I met Gordon March, you remember him, he used to be Manager of 5DN, and by jove didn't he look magnificent in his naval uniform. He was going to Port Adelaide to go aboard his mine-sweeper and he asked me to give you all his kind regards.'

Following the closure the government removed the station's license. The Church appealed to the High Court, but lost the case.

5KA reopened in December 1943, now owned by the Methodist Church and the Labour Party. By 1954, general opinion was that the Jehovah's Witness Church had been extremely hard done by. I understand that no compensation was ever paid.

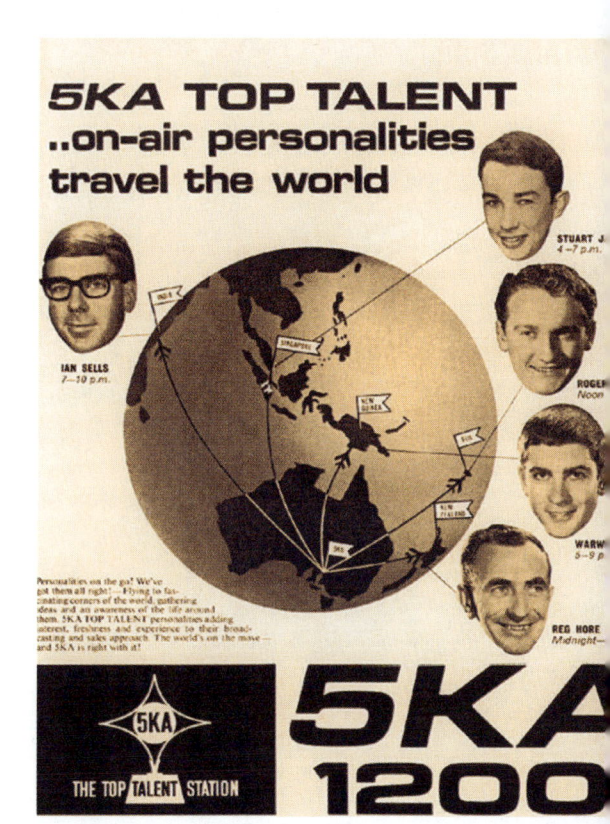

5KA personalities you might recall from the 1960s. By then the station was owned by the Methodist Church and the Australian Labor Party

*5KA/KAFM*

# #13
## FACT

Maslin Beach, 35 kilometres southwest of the city, in the Fleurieu Peninsula, is (in)famous as the state's and nation's first official nude beach. It hosts a 'Nude Olympics' annually.

1997

Darren Jarman throws his arms in the air after his fifth goal and the one that sealed the result of the Adelaide Crows grand final win in 1997

*Photo by News Ltd/Newspix*

It was an awesome day, the last Saturday in September 1997 when Malcolm Blight's Crows somehow managed to beat the red-hot favourites St Kilda and win their first-ever grand final in the AFL. East Rundle Street soon teamed with thousands of people who flocked into the city on the spur of the moment to celebrate the unexpected victory. Complete strangers hugged and kissed as the party lasted into the night. Adelaide went on to win the flag again in 1998, this time against North Melbourne.

# 1948

A devastating storm ripped through Adelaide in April 1948, destroying the Glenelg Jetty and driving the survey ship *Barcoo* aground.

The *Barcoo* was commissioned by the navy in 1944 and saw active service in New Guinea and Borneo, engaged in convoy escort duties. After the war it was put to work as a survey vessel and was involved in work off the coast of Glenelg when the storm struck in the early hours of that morning. The *Barcoo* dragged its anchor and ended up on the beach at Glenelg. It was stuck fast for more than a week while efforts were made to re-float her. Crowds of curious onlookers turned up every day until the ship was eventually re-floated and towed into Port Adelaide.

The *Barcoo* continued in service as a survey vessel until she was decommissioned and sold for scrap in February 1972.

The Barcoo Outlet, which allows stormwater to drain from the Patawolonga, is named after the vessel.

The survey ship *Barcoo* dragged anchor and was washed up on the beach at Glenelg after the storm of 1948

*Photo by Bill Krischock/Newspix*

# 1958

I had a friend who played the fife in a drum and fife band at another school. Our school played marching music over the loudspeaker and we marched to that. Many schools used to have an army cadet band and even army cadet units.

You would not even recognise this as Adelaide Oval now. The new football stadium is huge and very modern with all facilities. I loved the old cricket ground and it's a shame that we had to lose it, but I admit to enjoying the new venue.

Looks like the West Torrens and South Adelaide football teams were playing that day. That is when local footy reigned supreme!

Named after British Field Marshal Horatio Lord Kitchener, the Kitchener Bun is the World War I South Australian answer to the Berliner Bun

*Creative Commons*

'Many schools in the '50s had their own drum and fife band and this photo (taken by my father in August 1958) shows the Black Forest Primary School band which, aged 12, I had the pleasure of leading onto Adelaide Oval during half time of the football game', writes Ken Taylor

*Courtesy of Ken Taylor*

1966

A TAA aircraft just after landing on a wet Adelaide day in 1966 with passengers scurrying for the terminal. No 'skybridges' in those days
*Photo by News Ltd/Newspix*

For years Adelaide was seen as something of a backwater because of our airport terminal. At that time everyone arriving or departing by air had to walk across the tarmac to or from the plane.

Our award-winning international and domestic terminal opened in 2005. In 2006 it was designated 'the world's second-best internatonal airport' in the category serving between 5 and 15 million passengers. In 2006, 2009 and 2011 it was listed as Australia's 'best capital city airport'.

As for TAA, it eventually became Australian Airlines, owned and operated by Qantas, and closed in 1994.

1980

The Bay Sheffield is one of the great traditional sporting events held in South Australia every year. Paul Elliot celebrates as he storms across the line in first place to win the big prize in 1980

*Photo by Peter Watkins/Newspix*

The Bay Sheffield footrace has been held every year since 1887 on the day South Australia celebrates its birthday – December 28 (Proclamation Day). Every year thousands of people gather at Colley Reserve Glenelg for the annual event and cheer home the winner.

The race has a colourful history with many well-known SANFL footballers competing over the years and claiming victory, as well as a good number of athletes going on to success in the Stawell Gift. In the entire history of the event, entry has always been free, except in 1922 when the arena was closed off and a small fee charged with proceeds going to the building of a war memorial.

## 1959

Was life in Adelaide in the 1950s better, more fun and easier to manage than it is today? One of the great dangers of nostalgia is that we tend to look back at the past through rose-coloured glasses.

There is no doubt it was a more innocent time and life was simpler than it is today, but there was a dark side too. Many of the men who had returned from the World War II continued to struggle with their demons and there was little understanding of their suffering. Polio remained a constant threat and women were rarely given the opportunities or recognition they deserved.

Rundle Street traffic, east bound, 21 December 1959

*Photo by Pat Crowe/Newspix*

1959

## 1974

The Banana Room and Anthony's Fruit Palace in the east end of Rundle Street in 1977 with Sophie van Rood's left-hand Ford Thunderbird (brought from Curaçao in 1964 when she and her family migrated) parked outside. There was a flowers and vegetable seed shop over the road that may have been part of the old vegetable market

*Courtesy of Rob Wallace*

The Banana Room was Sophie van Rood's now famous vintage clothing shop where you could reportedly purchase beautiful clothes from all over the world for a fraction of what they would normally have cost.

Many of the clothes had been salvaged from deceased-estate auctions, op-shops, garage sales and even rubbish dumps. Some of the clothes were apparently so spectacular that about 25 items from the original shop are now displayed permanently at Sydney's Powerhouse Museum.

'Here's Sophie in the original Banana Room. I believe that when she and Tom Spender (my former husband) started The Banana Room in 1974, it was Australia's largest vintage emporium and ended up being one of the oldest collections when we closed the doors in 2002.'

*Courtesy of Candy Spender van Rood*

1977

At The Palais there was everything from ballroom dancing through to rock'n'roll concerts on a Saturday afternoon. The interior had a curved roof and it was a huge hall built in 1920 and serving as a popular location for dances and bands right through to 1967 when it was converted into the Palais Parking Station, before being demolished in 1972.

The Palais on North Terrace, 1967, just before it was converted into a parking station

*State Library of South Australia B16838/1*

1954

Were you there? When the Queen and the Duke of Edinburgh visited Adelaide in 1954, Adelaide school children were bussed to Wayville Showgrounds to welcome the royal pair

*Photo by News Ltd/Newspix*

Who can forget the Queen and Duke of Edinburgh's first visit back in 1954 when we welcomed the beautiful young queen and her handsome prince to Adelaide for the first time?

Reports from *The Advertiser* on that day, 18 March 1954, estimated a crowd of some 200,000 people had turned out for the start of the eight-day visit, with large numbers lining the route from Parafield Airport.

Later that week, at the Wayville showground, more than 100,000 children from schools all over the city gathered for a royal music festival to welcome Her Majesty. We practised for weeks at school to form part of a giant tableau which spelled out 'LOYALTY' and formed the crown. It was quite spectacular really and went without a hitch. After that we got to sit on the oval while other schoolchildren performed dances and other various acts depicting life in Australia.

# #14
## FACT

1981

Mount Lofty is well-known to visitors to Adelaide as a vantage point for panoramic views of the city. At night the lights of the city have a particular charm and it has always been a romantic destination.

Neil Hawke, remembered as a great sporting champion and for his prolonged battle with illness, shown here in 1981, when he was taken to Thebarton Oval, home of his much-loved West Torrens, where the crowd stood as one and cheered him

*Photo by News Ltd/Newspix*

Neil Hawke was a sporting all-rounder, taking 91 Test wickets in the 1960s. As an Aussie Rules footballer he kicked a bagful of goals in just his third league game and was a member of the legendary 1963 State team that beat the Vics at the MCG.

In 1980, complications from bowel surgery, including liver and kidney failure, almost killed him but he fought on, only to face another 30 operations and 12 cardiac arrests before his death on Christmas Day 2000, aged 61.

### 1958

In the '50s and '60s a birthday party was a neighbourhood event and on that special day there was a party at your house for the other kids in the street.

There would be fairy bread, chocolate crackles, little cakes in patty pans, raspberry cordial and of course the birthday cake made and iced by Mum (from real ingredients, not from a packet). There would be a little party hat for everyone, games too, and some of the other mums would be there to watch over 'Mr Wolf' and 'Pin the Tail on the Donkey' or 'Pass the Parcel'.

In my family we got to have our own party only once every four years (there were four kids in the family), but we all joined in each other's party as well.

'Gwen Adam made these fashionable cakes for my twin brother and my fifth birthday party in 1963'
*Courtesy of Di Quick*

Dale Phillips' brother's first birthday party in 1959 in Elizabeth – replete with well-wishers, fridge, stove and a smoking mum
*Courtesy Dale Phillips*

1 9 6 3

1961

The Dolphins Marching Girls team at the Royal Adelaide Show in 1961

*Photo by News Ltd/Newspix*

Marching girls were originally introduced into Australia in the 1930s but really started to take off in the late '50s. By the mid '60s there were national titles established and thousands of girls around Adelaide would proudly don their uniform and boots and march every week. *The Australian Women's Weekly* published an article about marching girls in Adelaide in June 1966: 'They march through the streets, at parks, in playing fields. They march at football matches, carnivals, Mardi Gras, and fetes. A festive occasion in Australia isn't complete without a team of marching girls these days ... Teams compete for medals and trophies, as well as the right to contest the Australian championships held every Easter.'

# 1971

In January 1971 thousands of music fans gathered for a long weekend of peace, love and rock'n'roll at a hot and dusty dairy farm 60 kilometres south of Adelaide.

Black Sabbath was there. So was Daddy Cool, Spectrum, Chain and although Billy Thorpe and the Aztecs didn't quite get there, it was still a memorable event. The Myponga Pop Festival was South Australia's answer to Woodstock. There was lots of booze and drugs and an 'anything goes' attitude that was not unusual at such an event.

The big crowd partied for three days and nights to the sounds of some of Australia's, and indeed the world's, best musical acts. Just another example of Adelaide leading the rest of Australia at that time.

Getting into the music at the Myponga Pop Music Festival

Photo by News Ltd/Newspix

## 1967

Don Dunstan has a beer in the bar of the Challa Gardens Hotel in West Croydon after 6 o'clock on the first night of 10pm closing, 1967

*Photo by Vern Thompson/Newspix*

Most of us are very familiar with 'the 6-o'clock swill', a term used to describe the mad rush to drink as many beers as possible before the hotel bar was forced to close with 'Time gentleman, please, last drinks!' Throughout much of the 20th century a culture developed of heavy drinking in the period between 'knock-off time' from work and the bar closure. It was as early as 1937 when Tasmania extended drinking hours, followed by New South Wales in the 1940s, and then the other mainland states. South Australia was the last to abolish 6-o'clock closing when Don Dunstan finally introduced legislation back in 1967, allowing pubs and clubs to serve alcohol until 10pm, with restaurants allowed to serve drinks with a meal until midnight.

# #15
## FACT

Sharks are more likely to be found on the menu at your local fish and chip shop (as 'flake'), but they occasionally attack and have killed 6 people at beaches in Adelaide since 1836, when the colony of South Australia was founded.

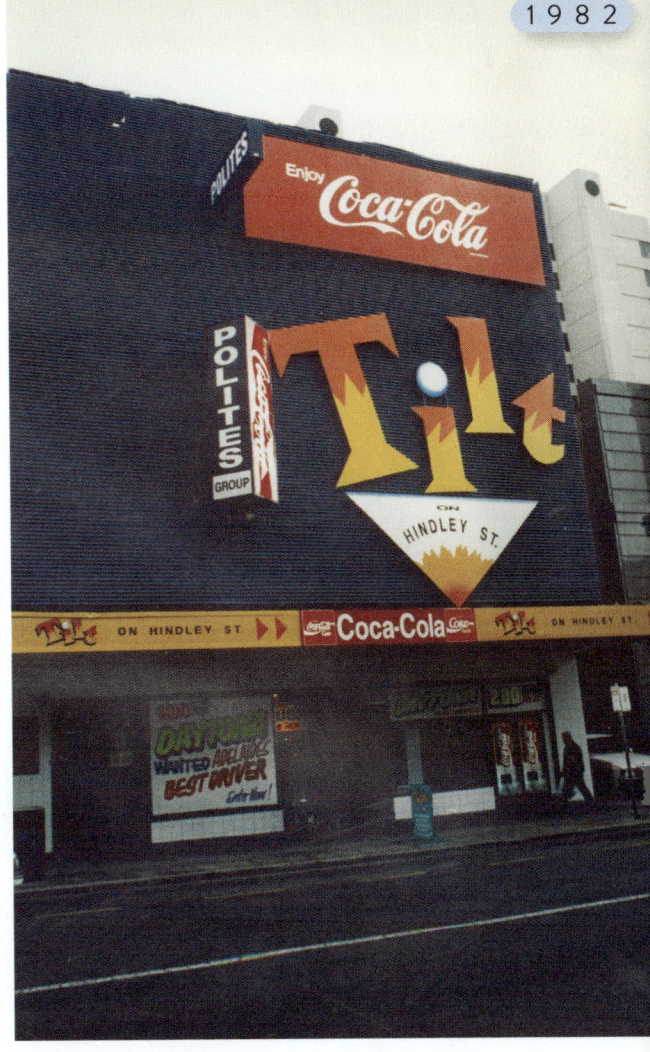

1982

Tilt in Hindley Street
*State Library of South Australia B71775/46*

Arcade games were really popular in Adelaide in the 1980s and in Hindley Street there were two places to go for a fun night out: Downtown, which was more family oriented and Tilt. Both offered a variety of activities and a good night out. The building that used to house Tilt is now divided into individual smaller shops.

## 1950

After the first Holden was released in Australia in 1948, parking stations suddenly mushroomed across the city. In the late 1960s when I was working at the old Advertiser building, I used to park in an open car park where the Topham Street multi-level car park now stands. In those days parking stations in and around the city were usually just a block of land with a pay station and a single operator.

Pump service was expected at most stations with Caltex and Mobil dominating the market, as in this shot taken in 1950 of Roberts Parking Station in Hindley Street. It obviously served both Caltex and Plume, which was the early name used by Mobil. What a fabulous range of period cars parked in the lot!

1950

Carpark 1950s style. Before we had multi-level carparks in the city, an empty block of land was all that was needed to create a parking station

*Photo by News Ltd/Newspix*

## 1955

Operators at the Central Exchange in Franklin Street, photographed on 13 May 1955, the day before the Exchange closed; left to right: Margie Matthew, who was a monitor; Mrs Nell Knight; Mrs Gwen Smith

*State Library of South Australia B62198*

Students in the early 1980s at Blackwood Junior Primary School using plastic buckets and containers for protection from the swooping maggies

*Photo by News Ltd/Newspix*

With the recent arrival of smart phones, it's difficult to believe how far we've come in the world of telephony. In my lifetime, I've seen the phone change from a simple instrument of communication, to a mini-computer complete with enough gadgets and gizmos to make your head spin! As a kid, I used to spend some of my school holidays on my great-aunt's farm near Quorn. Back in the '50s, they had no electricity, but did have a phone on a party line that they had to crank by hand. Then we moved to handsets, first without a dial, where you picked up the phone and would be put through to the exchange and asked 'Number, please'. Then came phones with their own dials, so you could directly dial the person you wanted to talk to. Even then for interstate and overseas calls you still had to go through the exchange.

The first mobile phones began to appear in the late 1980s, the size and weight of a house brick and they gradually got smaller and smaller until in 2007 the first iPhone appeared.

# 1982

Spring in Adelaide is magpie season, when breeding magpies around the suburbs become very aggressive (especially the males) and swoop to attack those who approach their nests, especially bike riders and kids in the playground. I recall at school being terrified of the maggies, appearing out of nowhere to give you a hell of a scare. When I was at primary school (in the years before plastic buckets) we held our school bags and school cases on our heads for protection.

Who remembers David Hookes' amazing century from 34 balls back in 1982 at the Adelaide Oval? Hookesy was apparently angry about the delayed finish to the Victorian innings by Graham Yallop; he promoted himself to the top of the order and took out that anger on the bowling. Although the match finished as a draw, it still remains today as the fastest first-class century of all time.

His tragic death in 2004, at age 48, left Adelaide in mourning. More than 10,000 fans attended a special memorial service for him at Adelaide Oval.

South Australian sports fans loved 'Hookesy'. David Hookes was one the finest cricketers this State has ever produced and a great bloke!

*Photo by News Ltd/Newspix*

## 1956

Adelaide's City Baths were built on the western side of King William Street and first opened in 1861. They operated there until 1969 when the Adelaide Aquatic Centre was opened in North Adelaide. The City Baths were then demolished with the location to be used for the Festival Centre complex.

In 1940, an Olympic-size swimming pool and high-diving facilities were added and it was during the 1950s that Olympic swimming coach Harry Gallagher took over the management of the baths and brought with him a young swimming star, Dawn Fraser, who trained for her Olympic campaigns at the Baths. Dawn made many friends while she was in Adelaide and many people can still remember watching her doing laps of the pool with Harry running alongside, stopwatch in hand, yelling out encouragement. The good old days!

On a hot January day in 1956 the Baths were an extremely popular place to be. There was a big 50-metre pool, a series of springboards and a very high diving platform

*Photo by News Ltd/Newspix*

# 1976

The Gerard family are well known in Adelaide through their business Clipsal Industries. The brand was first established in the 1920s and over the next 50 years expanded and prospered under the leadership of Geoff Gerard. Son Robert took over the reins in 1976 and decided to further expand the business into Asia, India, South Africa, the United Kingdom and Russia.

Hundreds of Adelaideans have worked at Clipsals over the years and although the Gerards decided to sell their stake in the business to a French company in 2004, it remains as an important industry for the city. Bob and his family still retain control of a number of companies that they accumulated over a number of years and continue to play a role in industry in Adelaide.

Robert Gerard, noted South Australian businessman and philanthropist

Photo by Mark Brake/Newspix

1951

*Baseball at the Norwood Oval under lights was a huge crowd-puller in the 1950s with thousands of fans turning up for the mid-week games*

Photo by News Ltd/Newspix

It's not unusual for the Norwood Oval to be packed with thousands of fans for the football, but for a time in the 1950s, Adelaide boasted a baseball game that drew its own crowds.

Many will remember the night games under lights during the hot Adelaide summers from 1951, with the South Australian Baseball team being tenants at the oval until 1988. During those years Norwood Oval hosted the Claxton Shield competition on six occasions with South Australia taking out the coveted trophy on at least four occasions.

# #16
## FACT

What a boulevard is North Terrace! On its north side alone are the Botanic Gardens, the Royal Adelaide Hospital, the Universities of South Australia and Adelaide, the Art Gallery of South Australia, the South Australian Museum, the State Library of South Australia, the Shrine of Remembrance, Government House, Parliament House, the Casino, the Railway Station, InterContinental Hilton and Adelaide Convention Centre.

1958

Dad's FJ taxi on Henley Beach Road at Torrensville, around 1958, parked outside the local deli

*Courtesy of Kenny Peplow*

The local corner shop, or deli, was the beating heart of many communities, as well as a source of local gossip and an income for the families who ran them. In a recent *Advertiser* article, History SA chief executive Margaret Anderson wrote:

> For most of Adelaide's history, the corner shop was an essential part of the community. It stocked many of the basic essentials – bread, milk, flour, sugar, newspapers and also cigarettes, once these became popular. What was more important was it sold them in small quantities – a little of almost everything – so that those with little money could afford to buy.

Who can recall a trip to the corner shop on a hot Adelaide evening for a cold bottle of Woodies Lemonade to share with the family, or purchasing 1/- worth of broken biscuits in a brown paper bag?

131

## 1958

Many people will recall the double-decker trolley buses, of course, but for a brief time we also had a fleet of diesel double-deckers too.

The last double-decker buses were taken off the road in the early 1960s. I have a recollection of double-decker buses going down Port Road and along Anzac Highway to Glenelg.

Waiting in July 1958 to catch the 5pm double-decker bus in King William Street (outside what is now the Bank SA building) to St Leonards (now Glenelg North). Note all the denting along the left-side roofline. Obviously it has been travelling a bit close to the trees!

*Photo by News Ltd/Newspix*

1936

Adelaide got its first set of traffic lights on the corner of King William, Hindley & Rundle Streets intersection in December 1927. They were a Swedish-made stop-go set with only red and green lights.

It wasn't until November 1936 that we got our first set of the three-colour system. Maybe we should have stuck to the two-light system, because Adelaide is the only place I know of where an amber light (normally a signal to slow down), means floor it!

The first set of automatic traffic lights, using the three-colour system, being installed in Adelaide by the Adelaide City Council Works Department at the King William Street/ North Terrace intersection in November 1936

*Photo by News Ltd/Newspix*

# 1954

Cars line up at the opening of our first drive-in picture theatre, the Blue Line Drive-In West Beach, 1954

*Photo by News Ltd/Newspix*

I loved going to the drive-in pictures. The 'Drive-In' phenomenon reached Adelaide in 1954 when the Blue Line Drive-In first opened on the corner of West Beach and Military Roads, West Beach, on 28 December. Press reports from that time show the excitement that the drive-in caused with 'tangled traffic scenes in the area when thousands of motorists tried to see the opening. Cars were queued for

1954

miles and many just parked outside on the side of the road hoping to watch the films from outside the fence'. Showing on the opening night was John Gregson, Kay Kendall and Kenneth Moore in the classic veteran car comedy *Genevieve*. The supporting program was a Heckle and Jeckle cartoon, newsreel and a featurette. And check out the Stobie poles, unique to South Australia.

Even garbage collection has gone hi-tech these days with the three-bin system (rubbish, recyclable and green waste) and just one person driving an air-conditioned truck. I recall there would be three or four garbos running up and down the street grabbing the old metal garbage bins and emptying the rubbish into the back of the old garbage truck. They'd start banging the bins at 5 in the morning, waking up the neighbourhood, the truck revving up the street and the guys yelling to one another.

At Christmas you would leave some beers out for the garbos. It would have been a bloody tough job, cold and wet in winter, stinking hot in summer and I can never recall any of the blokes wearing protective clothing either! OH&S would have a fit if they tried to do it today.

Garbos at work in Mitcham in the early 1980s. The garbage collection was done by blokes jumping off the truck and grabbing the old bins

Photo by News Ltd/Newspix

# 1960

Up until the early 1970s in some neighbourhoods, hot, fresh, crusty bread was delivered by horse and cart every day, right to your home. The horse got to know the route so well and knew when to stop, allowing the bread delivery man (or woman) to make four or five deliveries before returning to the cart to refill the big wicker bread basket and continue with delivery on foot.

If you were lucky there was sometimes a bonus of a fresh yeast finger bun or even a ride in the cart! And if Dad was lucky there was a bonus for him too … some fresh fertiliser left for the vegie patch!

*The daily bread delivery. Who can remember the smell of the hot fresh bread wafting up the street?*

*Photo by News Ltd/Newspix*

### 1962

As a kid in the 1950s and '60s a day at the beach was a real treat and apart from the inevitable dose of sunburn (no slip-slop-slap in those days), it was a great day out. I'm sure most people will recall the sandcastle-building competitions. They were pretty serious affairs and some contestants got to the beach early to stake out a claim for the right bit of sand: not too wet and not too dry. There were cash prizes for the winner too!

*The Advertiser* sandcastle competition senior winner Susan Butler (left) with junior winner Carolyn Bland, congratulated by Port Adelaide mayor Mr P Whicker in 1962

*Photo by News Ltd/Newspix*

1972

# #17
## FACT

For years parents had it easy getting the kids to bed. At 7.30pm, Channel 10's Fat Cat would say 'Goodnight, boys and girls' and children would dutifully go off to bed

*Photo by News Ltd/Newspix*

Adelaide TV station Channel 10 introduced the idea of Fat Cat saying goodnight to the children at 7.30pm every night. It was the time when the station drew a line and said the programs after this time may not be suitable for children. And the children of the day accepted that when Fat Cat went to bed they were quite happy to do the same. I think Fat Cat said 'Goodnight' for the final time not long after SAS 10 became SAS 7. His show was axed in 1992 because the Australian Broadcasting Tribunal said the character was confusing and the show wasn't educational.

Is it true that there is an Adelaide accent? Yes, but only just. Variations in the Australian accent are slight because the population has moved around a lot over 200 years of European settlement and this surging movement has levelled out our accent. Some would say Adelaide leans towards being posh, with people here more likely to say 'daahnce' or 'plaahnts'. But the differences are very slight.

# 1963

*Wikipedia*

Theatre Royal, 1955. Demolished by Miller Andersons to make way for a car park!

*State Library of South Australia B13215*

Following the demise of the regular tram system, trolley buses took over most of the routes. Actually trolley buses were first introduced into Adelaide back in the late 1930s and continued to operate until about 1963 when the last line was converted to motor buses.

My strongest recollection of the old double-decker trolley buses is that they had both a front and rear entrance and that the rear entrance had no door, so if you got to the stop, just as the trolley bus was pulling away, you could grab the pole and haul yourself on board, sometimes with the helping hands of other passengers and even the conductor. Not something that would be allowed these days, I'm sure.

The other strong memory is the big hooks on the back of the buses. When a woman with a pram got onto the bus, she would leave her pram on the footpath and once all the other passengers were on board the driver or conductor would get off the bus and go and hang the pram on one of the big hooks.

1955

The Theatre Royal in Hindley Street was demolished in 1962. Hard to believe that anybody would do such a thing! The Theatre Royal was Adelaide's best-known and most-loved theatre. Many historic events occurred here, including the first moving picture show in Adelaide in 1896 and appearances by such famous performers as Sarah Bernhardt, Katherine Hepburn and the Oliviers. The loss of such gems reminds us we need to have more sense, more pride and more appreciation of our history!

1953

# 1971

Remember in the 1950s and 1960s: shops were open from 9am to 5.30pm on weekdays and 9 to 11.30 on Saturdays. There was no late-night shopping, no shops open on public holidays and no Sunday trading. How on earth did we survive?

Here is Rundle Street in 1953 crowded with people doing their last-minute Christmas shopping. Birks Department store, first opened in Hindley Street in 1864. In the 1880s it moved to Rundle Street, which at the time was a thoroughfare still used by vehicle traffic until it was turned into a mall in 1976. Birks was bought by David Jones in the mid to late 1950s and DJ's still stands in that location today.

*Courtesy of Mort Hansen*

Mort Hansen shared a photo and some memories: 'Here's my school bank book from 1971. There's still $1.40 in it! I'm guessing the surfboard is about the only thing a school kid might save for these days.'

I recall that Mondays were 'bank' days at my primary school in the 1950s and we would take our bank books and 6d and our school money of 2/- (that was for the nuns). I could never really see any point in saving money, when I could have put that 6d to good use buying lollies or chewies! I think the cover of my bank book was more of a dark grey in colour, with pages inside having figures written in the columns and little stamped entries.

Memories from a long time ago!

Christmas Shopping in Rundle Street 1953 style. No late-night trading or longer shopping hours on the weekend

*Photo by News Ltd/Newspix*

1963

1963

The old Central Methodist Mission building, which also housed Radio 5KA, on the corner of Franklin and Pitt Streets in 1963
*State Library of South Australia B15296*

The Central Methodist Mission was a prominent site in Franklin Street, but was demolished in about 1964 to be replaced by the new Central Mission with the Maughan Methodist Church, as well as Radio Station 5KA. The new complex still stands on the site today.

# 1959

Ozone Theatre at Marryatville

*Photo by News Ltd/Newspix*

Did you go to the Saturday afternoon matinee at your local picture theatre? Our photo is the Ozone (just recently bulldozed) in Jetty Road, Glenelg, and there were also Hoyt's Ozones in Enfield, Semaphore, Unley, Alberton, Colonel Light Gardens, Goodwood, Henley Beach, Marryatville (which become the Chelsea, then the Regal), Port Adelaide, Prospect and Unley. There were Odeon Stars (now Piccadilly) at North Adelaide, Goodwood, Hindmarsh, Port and Norwood, Unley, Semaphore, Thebarton, Parkside, St Peters, Glenelg and Kilkenny. There was the Roxy, Vogue and the Cinema Curzon (Capri). We had the Windsor pictures at Brighton, St Morris, Lockleys and Hilton. There were picture theatres at Dulwich and Findon and in the city The Regent, York, Majestic, Royal, Rex, Civic, Wests, Metro and the newsreel theatre The Savoy. I'm sure I've missed a few as well.

# 1955

Not a lot of people will remember parking meters because we were too young to drive. Now of course we do and parking meters are now machines that gobble up money and dispense a ticket to put on your dashboard.

Legislation for the meters was introduced in 1955 and a 'promotional' meter was installed outside Wests Theatre in Hindley Street in August with all the proceeds going to the Adelaide Children's Hospital. The old-style parking meters didn't really take over the streets until 1958 when 90 were installed and a cost for parking in the city has been with us ever since.

Adrienne Fleming puts a shilling into Adelaide's first parking meter in 1955

*Photo by News Ltd/Newspix*

1960

Traffic at the busy intersection of Rundle and Hindley Streets being directed by a police officer, Constable N. Calvin, in 1960

*Photo by Barry O'Brien/Newspix*

Many older South Australians will recognise this police officer, who used to be almost a fixture at the intersections of North Terrace and/or Hindley/Rundle Streets at King William Street back in the 1960s. No matter what day we were ever in the city, he always seemed to be there, directing traffic with his classic pose of whistle up to his mouth and pointing at something or someone. Even though traffic signals had been installed, Constable Calvin remained at his post!

# #18
## FACT

Often known as 'The City of Churches', Adelaide actually is one of the less religious cities in the country, but it has a reputation for tolerance (hence the variety of spiritual places, be they church, mosque, synagogue or temple)

1950

Pulteney Street looking south from North Terrace in 1950

State Library of South Australia B67020

Scots Church on North Terrace is in the foreground with Ruthven Mansions directly behind, both still to be found in the Adelaide of today. You can clearly make out the tram tracks that ran the full length of Pulteney Street in those days. On the left of the photo, the large building was Foy and Gibsons (previously Grand Central Hotel) now demolished and replaced with the Rundle Street Car Park and in front of that would have been Cravens Department Store, now Centrepoint.

## 1981

The MV *Troubridge* was originally put into service by RW Miller in 1961, and in later years was run as a joint venture with the South Australian Government. MV *Troubridge* was used mainly on the Kangaroo Island trip to Kingscote and was a roll-on, roll-off vessel of 1996 tons. It operated until 1 June 1987, when it was replaced by the Government-run $23 million *Island Seaway*, which turned out to be a bit of a disaster. On the inaugural trip, seventy-five sheep and cattle died due to carbon monoxide poisoning, and the ship was once described as 'steering like a shopping trolley'.

The MV *Troubridge* in 1981
*State Library of South Australia*
*Photograph by Jenny Scott*

1966

Field umpire (only had one then), Ken Cunningham keeping Sturt's Malcolm Hill (left), skipper John Halbert and Port Adelaide's Bob Clayton in check in the 1966 Grand Final at Adelaide Oval

Photo by News Ltd/Newspix

Local footy used to be played only on a Saturday afternoon. All games started at approximately the same time and there were no Friday night games or Sunday football. Football belonged to the supporters and players cared more about the jumper than the money. I recall going with my father to the local league games in the late 1950s and early 1960s and being allowed to wander into the clubrooms at half time to smell the liniment and to see the players being rubbed down by the trainers.

We were allowed to run onto the oval at three-quarter time for a kick and listen to the coach exhorting his players (who were sucking on a quarter orange) to give it their all in the final quarter. They were the days when coaches and players didn't worry about the press, yet players became household names, even before TV broadcasts and endless Sunday morning footy panel shows.

## 1984

On Australia Day 1984 an all-day concert was staged at Colley Reserve in Glenelg. It was hot and many people in the crowd had been drinking for most of the day. As night fell some people in the crowd started an ice fight, which initially was just in fun, but after a while several fights broke out and a riot erupted with the big crowd completely out of control.

Police barricaded themselves into the police station in Moseley Square until back-up arrived. Police cars were torched and 63 people were arrested. The riot led to the foreshore becoming a 'dry area'. It did however spawn some pretty good T-shirts, like 'Come to Glenelg ... it's a riot.'

A girl being arrested after the Glenelg riot in 1984 that erupted during a concert in the Colley Reserve

*Photo by News Ltd/Newspix*

I worked in the 5KA Mobile Studio at the Royal Adelaide Show in 1969

*5KA/KAFM*

In the golden days of radio, there were mobile studios that businesses could engage for a hefty fee to run a promotion broadcast from its premises, with the on-air personality presenting his program 'live'. This is a photo of the 5KA mobile studio, probably in the late '60s. From memory 5DN and 5KA had mobiles but I don't believe 5AD ever had one.

Do you remember such great radio jocks as Chas ('big C little h a s') Lumsden, Jim Slade, Roger Dowsett, Stuart Jay, Bill Long, Tony Phillips, Ian Sells and later Lawrie Bruce, Dave Whitcombe, Jeff Warden and Barry Bissell? All would at some stage have broadcast live from this van.

**2006**

The Hills Hoist is a great South Australian invention! And, not only for getting the washing dried, but for kids to hang on to and go for a whizzy. The Hills Hoist was first developed in Glenunga, by Lance Hill in 1945. It's described as a 'rotary clothesline that can be raised and lowered by a winding mechanism. This feature, in addition to the rotating square frame, allows the washing to dry more effectively in the breeze. The Hills Hoist also makes the most of limited space in suburban backyards. Hills celebrated the sale of the five millionth Hills Hoist in 1994 and now exports the clothesline around the world. The Hills Hoist has become an Australian suburban icon.'

A Hill's Hoist in the backyard of Wanbrow Avenue, Wattle Park. This is a quintessential Australian backyard with the Hill's Hoist, the galvanised-iron rainwater tank and the shed

*State Library of South Australia B70036*

1955

Adelaide in 1955 when Dad and Mum would dress in their Sunday best to go to town. A day out shopping in the city at that time generally meant a hat and gloves for ladies, while gentlemen wore a suit and tie. This photo was taken at 11am on Remembrance Day, when the whole city literally stopped to recall the end of hostilities of World War I. People stepped out of their cars, some halfway across intersections, and stood in silence to honour the fallen.

1955

Lots of great old cars in this photo. On the left the National Mutual building and on the right, something you won't see anymore, a tobacconist shop and behind that the Royal Exchange Hotel, demolished in the mid 1960s.

11 am on 11 November 1955: People observe a minute's silence for Remembrance Day on the corner of King William Street and Hindley Street

*Photo by Bob Cunningham/Newspix*

1977

# #19
## FACT

As in so many cities worldwide, Adelaide has a Chinatown. Its distinctive *paifang* (gates) indicate where to find it on Moonta Street, within the Adelaide Central Markets.

Sir Douglas Nicholls was the first Aboriginal person to be appointed to regal office when he became Governor of South Australia on 1 December 1976.

He began life on a reserve in New South Wales and at 13 started out as a tar boy on sheep stations. A gifted athlete, he was recruited by Carlton Football Club in the VFL, but due to the racist attitudes of the time, he did not play. He did play for the Northcote amateur league however and was a member of their 1929 premiership team. In 1932 he was back in the VFL, this time for Fitzroy and came third in the Brownlow Medal count in 1934. Knee problems forced him to retire from the game in 1939.

In 1935 Doug had taken a renewed interest in religion and social work and throughout the war years worked closely with the Fitzroy Aboriginal community, caring for those trapped in alcohol abuse, gambling and social problems. His work was so successful that he eventually became the pastor of the first Aboriginal Church of Christ in Australia.

This led him on to many other fine achievements until, in 1970, he was invited to be among guests to greet Queen Elizabeth II on her visit to Australia, and in 1972 became the first Aboriginal person to be knighted.

Sir Douglas Nicholls' inauguration as Governor of South Australia, 1977

*Courtesy of National Archives of Australia*

1977

1967

# 1967

Adelaide's iconic chocolate-maker Haighs is about to celebrate its 100th anniversary. Alfred Haigh started the business on 1 May 1915 when he opened his first shop on the Beehive Corner on King William and Rundle Streets.

Since then the business has thrived and 13 more shops have been opened around Australia. Alister Haigh, Alfred's grandson, recalls as a child, pocketing handfuls of chocolate treats when visiting his father, John, at the factory in Parkside. 'I have that memory of going to the factory with my mother after school and grabbing some of the chocolates,' he said. Alister is now chief executive of the famous South Australian brand.

As exhibits for the planned 100th anniversary celebration, Haighs has a Model-T Ford exact replica of the delivery van used in the 1920s and chocolate trays, used to carry Haigh's ice-cream at Mt Gambier's King Theatre back in 1905.

Beehive Corner, for 100 years the home of Haigh's quality chocolate and a real Adelaide icon. 'Meet you at the Beehive corner'!

*State Library of South Australia B17064*

## 1962

How many of us spent all day exploring the world with our best mate? Kenny Peplow at West Beach, 1962

*Courtesy of Kenny Peplow*

When I was growing up there were not many pedigree dogs in my neighbourhood, but plenty of bitsa's. They came from neighbours or friends who had pups to give away. Nobody ever seemed to buy a dog. And I'm struggling to remember whether dogs ever had any vaccinations back then, I don't recall my dogs ever being taken to the vet.

We had a family dog that died when it got the mange, and I had two dogs after that: Rex, a cross-border collie; and Rusty, a red kelpie bitsa. We'd roam all over the neighbourhood and beyond on our bikes and our dogs would run with us – how they were not run over by a car I'll never know.

No poodles or spoodles then, no tinned dog food either, just scraps from the butcher. I recall my mother cooking shanks and blade bones for the dogs to chew. And our dogs were never allowed inside at all.

1973

The first City–Bay fun run shows a group of keen amateurs just after the start of the race in 1973

Photo by News Ltd/Newspix

In November 1973, Bob Clarke, along with a volunteer committee established the first City–Bay Fun Run in Adelaide with *The News* newspaper and Coca-Cola as the first major sponsors.

The event started at the Adelaide Town Hall with 1600 enthusiastic runners who had each paid 50 cents to enter the 11.5 kilometre run that finished at the Glenelg Town Hall, opposite Moseley Square. Funds raised for the event were donated to Athletics South Australia.

Over the years there have been many changes to both starting and finishing lines and *The Sunday Mail* became the major sponsor in 1992. The City–Bay has become one of the biggest and best fun runs in Australia with a national profile. It attracts elite runners, international entrants and competitors from all over Australia – some 30,000 annually.

# 1956

Adelaide Oval was long regarded as the prettiest cricket ground anywhere in the world, but was also home to Australian Rules Football until Football Park was opened in 1974.

In the background is The John Creswell Stand, which was demolished to make way for the Sir Donald Bradman Stand in 1990, which has now all been demolished to make way for the new Football Stadium.

A predominantly male crowd is so enthralled during a semi-final between Norwood and North Adelaide that it completely ignores the young pie-seller in the foreground, 1956

*Photo by News Ltd/Newspix*

1973

Coopers, the local brew since 1862
*Creative Commons*

The Hayward family were associated with one of Adelaide's most-loved institutions, John Martins department store, from 1876. Edward Hayward was educated at St Peter's College and joined the family business in 1931.

One of his first duties was to visit North America and gather ideas from department stores in the USA and Canada. The plan for his most enduring legacy, the Adelaide Christmas Pageant, came from that first trip. South Australia was still recovering from the Great Depression and Hayward wanted to create an event that would help people smile again. He conceived the idea of a parade of floats based on fairytales and nursery rhymes with marching bands escorting Father Christmas to John Martins. Since the first Adelaide Christmas Pageant was held in 1933 it has become a much-loved annual tradition.

Sir Edward was a great lover of art and built up a world-class collection of works that he bequeathed to the state, along with his home 'Carrick Hill'. In 1973 he was recognised as South Australian Father of the Year, despite having no children, for his role in bringing so much joy to the children of Adelaide with the Christmas Pageant. He died in 1983.

Sir Edward Hayward gets into the spirit of things, clowning around with British actor John Inman from the hit TV series *Are You Being Served*
*Photo by News Ltd/Newspix*

## 1977

Remember public telephone boxes?
*Courtesy of Michael Brodie*

So, this is how we survived before mobile phones! Public phone boxes were on every second or third corner around the suburbs of Adelaide all through our growing up years, as well as in all the country towns.

My first job was as a telegram boy with the PMG Department and one of the jobs I had to do was ride a bike around to clear the 'boxes'. Sometimes the money boxes were full and very heavy and would have had a considerable amount of money in them as most people didn't have the phone on in the late 1950s and 1960s and used these public telephones.

Wests Picture Theatre was on the south side of Hindley Street and was a well-known Adelaide picture theatre. Built in 1939 and closed in 1977, the site remained largely vacant for some years. In 2001 the building was returned to its former glory retaining many of its art deco features, in particular the grand staircase that leads up to a mezzanine level in the entrance foyer. It now houses the Adelaide Symphony Orchestra, so continues its links to the past as an entertainment venue.

Wests Picture Theatre in Hindley Street in 1977
*State Library of South Australia B29909*
*Photo Ronald Praite, courtesy of John Praite*

## 2013

Semaphore Carousal is a well-known Adelaide icon, having entertained generations of children

*Photo by James Elsby/Newspix*

2013 was the 75th anniversary of the Semaphore Carousel. It is believed to be the largest operating carousel in Australia with 40 handcrafted wooden horses. The carousel is housed in an undercover enclosure to protect it from the elements and has been a favourite over the decades for families holidaying at the beach.

# 1950

Flower Day was once an Adelaide annual spring event. Each year from 1938 to the late 1960s the city was decorated with millions of blooms. The colourful and perfumed exhibits attracted tens of thousands of people and were held at various locations within the city square mile. The crowds would admire the floral carpet and other displays made up of thousands of flowers donated from town and country gardens around South Australia.

Spring 1950: thousands of people gather in Victoria Square for the annual Flower Day

*Photo by News Ltd/Newspix*

1950

1950

# 1950

Adelaide Railway Station was once the centre of all train travel in South Australia and the man in blue knew everything about anything to do with travelling on a train.

It was in 1978 that the South Australia's railway system was divided between two owners. The Commonwealth-government-controlled Australian National Railways (AN) took over ownership and operation of all country lines outside the Adelaide metropolitan area, while the State-government-controlled State Transport Authority (STA) retained the suburban routes around Adelaide, including ownership and operation of Adelaide Railway Station. By 1984 AN had moved to Keswick and in 1985 the ASER development program commenced and large areas of the Railway Station were converted into the casino.

'Ask the man in blue.' Look at that departure board. At mid century Adelaide Railway Station was the hub of travel

*Photo by News Ltd/Newspix*

1964

# #20
## FACT

Melbourne Street, North Adelaide, is a great place to wander among boutique shops, galleries or go for a meal, a coffee or a brew. There's the The Lion Hotel, which started off as a brewery, or round the corner the atmospheric British Hotel in Finniss Street.

In the same year that the Beatles came to town, Donald Campbell thrilled a big crowd outside the Adelaide Town Hall in his *Bluebird*

*Photo by News Ltd/Newspix*

Donald Campbell came to South Australia in 1964 with his *Bluebird* jet-powered car and set the world land-speed record of 403.1 mph (650km/h) on Lake Eyre. Afterwards he paraded his incredibly impressive and now famous sleek car in Adelaide. A huge crowd gathered to see Campbell drive his machine along King William Street to the Town Hall on 25 July 1964. He revved the engine to a huge roar sending the crowd wild.

Donald Campbell died three years later when his jet-powered boat, also named *Bluebird*, disintegrated at high speed as he tried to beat the world water-speed record. His body was not found until 2001.

1975

Ernie Sigley's final night hosting *Adelaide Tonight*. After almost a decade as one of the hosts of the show, Ernie returned to Melbourne in about 1975. From left singer Denis Walter, Helen Woods, unknown, then Ernie, Glenys O'Brien, Ian Fairweather and Anne Wills

*Courtesy of Channel 9*

*Adelaide Tonight* was a locally produced TV variety show on NWS 9 and was broadcast live from Studio 1 between 1959 and 1973. That's a lot of local television, and a lot of local talent would have been required to fill the many variety spots.

The comperes and presenters on the show were Lionel Williams, Kevin Crease, Ernie Sigley, Ian Fairweather, Gerry Gibson, Roger Cardwell and Anne Wills. Lionel stayed on local TV for many years; Kevin Crease went on to become one of Adelaide's best-known news readers; Ernie moved to Melbourne where he joined GTV 9; Ian Fairweather took on the role of Children's Programs in Sydney; Gerry Gibson, not sure; Roger had a fabulous career on radio and in voiceover work; and Willsy was on TV for many years after *Adelaide Tonight*.

The show produced some of Adelaide's best-known TV and radio personalities over many years!

1966

City Bowl was a great little bowling centre with a mezzanine coffee shop where you could sit and look out over the lanes while having a coffee and a toasted sandwich and waiting for your bowling time slot to come around.

Warren Burt recalls playing Thunderbird League at 9pm Thursday nights there for several years: 'It was the most friendly bowl in Adelaide in my opinion. The Dixon brothers, Angie, Mike and Nick with Barry de Boar made it a very personal experience. They knew all the bowlers and would greet them by name.'

I also remember the Bayside Bowl in Glenelg, which was the first ten-pin bowling alley in Adelaide back in the late 1950s, Woodville Bowl and Norwood Bowl.

The City Bowl was in Hindley Street and was very popular in the 1960s and beyond
*State Library of South Australia B71768/23 Messenger Press photo*

# 1969

The site of the Adelaide Hilton International Hotel with Hi-Fi Fashions on the corner, and with Moores Department store in the background

*Frank Hall, courtesy of Elaine Hall*

**1969**

The date of this photo is unknown but is most likely the late 1960s. The Hilton was opened at this location in October 1982 and Moores Department Store closed in the late 1970s and was purchased by the State Government in 1979 and opened as the Sir Samuel Way Building in 1983.

I recall there was much excitement when it was announced that the Hilton was coming to Adelaide. It cost $44 million to complete and it was Adelaide's first five-star hotel.

Looks like Hi-Fi Fashion had closed by the time this photo was taken, but some of the other businesses in the group of shops were still trading. After demolition the block may have been used as a parking lot before the hotel was finally constructed.

Note the lady crossing the road, all dressed up in Sunday-best, complete with hat and gloves. That's how I remember people dressed to 'go to town'.

## 1950

Did you have to force yourself to drink milk at school?

In 1950 the Australian Government introduced a scheme for school children to receive free milk. Every morning at about 9am, a small bottle of milk (1/3 pint, to be precise) would be delivered for each child. The milk would sit there (often in the sun) until morning recess, when each child would get their very own (now warm and possibly slightly off) bottle of milk.

The idea was that it would ensure that all Australian children would be getting fresh milk and a good dose of calcium each day. The idea was fine, but in practice there were a few problems. No refrigeration was available, but the teacher made you drink the milk, off or not. Milk delivery continued nationally from 1950 through to 1973 in most primary schools and even today there are many people who cannot stand the sight, smell or taste of milk.

Every day at school you would have to chug down a small bottle of milk. Put my wife off milk for years after

Photo by News Ltd/Newspix

**1960**

In 1958 a bicycle loving 15-year-old, Mick Harley, convinced his local council to grade a track for cycling races on a vacant block. That track on Reserve Parade in Findon is still the home to the 'Findon Skid Kids' and their Cycle Speedway. The Skid Kids started out as a bunch of daredevil young bicycle riders performing tricks and racing round the track just like these riders in this photo taken in 1960. Over the years thousands of young people have joined and the Findon Skid Kids have become famous all over Australia. The group are very active and have a strong and dedicated following. Were you ever a member of Findon Skid Kids?

Off to the zoo: Popeye on the River Torrens
*Creative Commons*

The Findon Skid Kids started in 1958. Since that time thousands of young kids have joined and the club still enjoys a very healthy membership today

*Photo by News Ltd/Newspix*

## 1970

The South had a wonderful history in Adelaide. A hotel was first built on the site in 1879 and then demolished and a more opulent building was erected in its place in 1893. It was upgraded again in 1899 adding a grand staircase and balcony. It remained as one of our grandest hotels until 1971 when it was bulldozed to make way for what is now the Stamford Plaza.

I was once told that the reason they had to demolish it was because it had 'concrete cancer' – the concrete gradually breaks down over time and the building becomes unsafe. I am not sure whether that was true or not. Or was The South simply a victom of that stupid era Adelaide went through in the 1960s and '70s where anything that had any history, or looked as though it might be worth preserving for the future, was knocked over!

The South Australian Hotel. Whenever the discussion turns to buildings that should never have been demolished, The South Australian Hotel is always on the list

*Frank Hall, courtesy of Elaine Hall*

1958

Peoplestores, another Adelaide department store that closed during the 1980s

*State Library of South Australia B17050*

At its peak, Adelaide was home to quite a number of department stores including Harris Scarfe, John Martins, Peoplestores, Miller Anderson, Cravens, Foy & Gibson (which later became Cox Foys and was eventually acquired by Harris Scarfe and closed in 1977), Charles Birks and Charles Moore's.

Peoplestores was founded in 1905 by owner W.H. Williams and expanded several times on the same site in Gouger Street. Six country stores also opened and in its heyday people flocked to the department store, which was quite close to Charles Moore's. After having traded for around eight decades, Peoplestores would cease all operations in South Australia during the 1980s. The large Gouger Street store was demolished and incorporated into various Central Market redevelopment schemes.

1997

## 1997

It was a very exciting moment in 1997 when the Adelaide Crows finally clinched the win over St Kilda and won their first AFL Grand Final. On the spur of the moment we drove into town and the whole city was literally jumping with joy with impromptu parties and celebrations in Rundle Street east and in Hindley Street. A few days later tens of thousands of people gathered in King William Street for a parade to welcome home the winning team with a presentation at the Adelaide Town Hall of the players and successful coach, Malcolm Blight. Adelaide's Premiership win is considered to this day one of the great sporting moments in Adelaide's history, setting off wild celebrations in the city. The Power won their first AFL Grand Final in 2004, beating Brisbane Lions.

Amazing scenes outside Adelaide Town Hall as the Crows were given a reception no-one will ever forget after their surprise premiership win in 1997

Photo by Barry O'Brien/Newspix

## 1962

Remember finishing work in the city around 5 or 5.30pm, rushing to catch the bus, tram or train and buying a copy of the late edition *Advertiser* or the afternoon paper, *The News*, from the paper boy who was standing on the footpath yelling out the day's headlines? In the 1960s, when this photo was taken, journalists wrote the stories, advertising sold the ads, newsagents and paper boys on street corners sold the papers.

These days it's much more complicated with newspapers now an on-line product, where news is updated every few minutes. Breaking news continues online 24 hours a day, people download the paper onto their iPad or tablet to read on the train or bus, subscribers now get a customer number, there's direct debit payment systems, newspapers run their own delivery agents. I often think about how much simpler it was before the advent of the computer when the paper was sold on the street corner.

'Read all about it … union leaders defied at mass meetings, get all the latest on the strikes. Read all about it!'

*Photo by News Ltd/Newspix*

# 1975

Adelaideans turned up in their thousands to watch the Birdman Rally every year from 1975 until 1986. The aim was to build a craft that would fly 50 metres or more.

When the first Birdman Rally was held in April 1975 on the River Torrens, some 25 000 people came to have a good laugh. The day turned into one of our favourites.

The Birdman Rally moved to Glenelg in 1976 and stayed there for the next ten years. As the event grew, so too did the sophistication of some of the craft that were entered. $10 000 was on offer for anyone, other than a hang-glider pilot, who could fly a distance of 50 metres, which by the way, I don't believe was ever achieved.

Birdman rallies took off around the country after the success of the Adelaide event and they still hold a birdman rally as part of Moomba in Melbourne each year. There was talk that it could come back to Glenelg, and there was a Facebook page started to get it going again, so who knows?

Noel O'Connor from Channel 10 with another contestant for The Birdman Rally

*Courtesy of Noel O'Connor*

1961

Mothers with their pre-school toddlers line up in 1961 to have their children vaccinated. Note that parking in those days was allowed in the centre of the road in Wakefield Street

*Photo by News Ltd/Newspix*

One of the great fears for parents in the 1950s and 1960s was polio. In 1961 the government established a nationwide immunisation program and I recall as a kid at school, lining up outside the school hall to get a 'needle'.

In that year there were 3 polio deaths and almost 30 cases. Here we see the first day of the emergency vaccination program when more than 2500 children were immunised at a mobile unit in the grounds of St Francis Xavier's Cathedral in Wakefield Street. The queue extended to the southern end of Victoria Square!

# 1961

This is still one of Adelaide's best-known and most successful small businesses, Miss Gladys Sym Choon's shop in east Rundle Street. The shop was originally The China Gift Shop and was opened by Gladys back in the 1920s. She came from a business family that had the monopoly in South Australia for the sale of fireworks and started her own business when she was just 18.

She became the first woman in Adelaide to import goods for sale and to form a business in her own right. She travelled extensively to China both for business and for family reasons and stocked her unique shop with all sorts of wonderful oriental treasures. In 1979 the business was passed to Gladys' daughter, Mei Ling, but was closed in 1985. When the current owners bought the shop they renamed it Miss Gladys Sym Choon.

The China Gift Shop in 1961

*State Library of South Australia B14563*

## 1984

*Kevin Crease, Lionel Williams and Ernie Sigley kick off the 1984 Channel 7 Good Friday Appeal*

State Library of South Australia B70869/14073 Messenger Press photo

The 5AD/Channel 7 Good Friday Appeal originally started out as just the 5AD Good Friday Appeal. A clipping from *The Advertiser* on 19 April 1954 reported that 'donations to the 5AD Good Friday Appeal this year raised a record of £27,520/15/10, for the Adelaide Children's Hospital building fund. Donations may be handed in at the front office of *The Advertiser* from 9am tomorrow. The manager of 5AD (Mr Keith Macdonald) said that it had been a wonderful result and thanked the listeners who had sent in donations.'

In 1969 it expanded to the 5AD/Channel 7 Good Friday Appeal and each year media personalities, performers and the public pitched in to raise millions of dollars over the years for the hospital. It was all totally unscripted television with a panel, usually including a major personality, reading out donations, with regular crosses to the phone room where the donations were being called through. People would be shaking collection cans at traffic lights and some people pulled some crazy stunts to raise money for the day.

# 1957

Ken Taylor shared a photo and a memory with us on 'Adelaide Remember When';

This photo of the Christmas Pageant was taken by my father on 9th November 1957 and shows the Adelaide Drum and Fife Band, of which I was a member at the time. The old 5AD building was replaced shortly after this by *The Advertiser* Building from which was broadcast 'Kangaroos on Parade' from the 10th floor. (This building has also since been replaced by the current building on the site.)

The old 5AD building was demolished to make way for the new 11-storey Advertiser Building that opened in 1960, only to be demolished in about 2007 and replaced by the ANZ Bank Building. Here we see another building next to the 5AD building (would that have been demolished along with the 5AD building?). The next building along is Electra House and there's the old Criterion Hotel, also now demolished.

Snow White and the Seven Dwarves, 2004

*Creative Commons*

1957 John Martin's Christmas Pageant marches along King William Street and passes the old Radio 5AD building, eventually demolished for the new Advertiser Building in 1960

*Courtesy of Ken Taylor*

1955

# #21
## FACT

Adelaide's most famous jetty is at Glenelg at the end of, appropriately, Jetty Road. In December, you might find the 2 Jetties Fun Run competitors slogging the 8.4 kilometres from there to Brighton Jetty. There are plenty more jetties along the Adelaide shoreline including Grange, Henley and Port Noarlunga.

Dorothy Chamberlain instructs her class on the art of standing straight with the help of a small beanbag (or sandbag) balanced on the head, 1955
*ARW*

1955

I do not recall being taught this sort of thing at school. The girls in our class used to have to walk with a book balanced on their head, but I don't think the boys were taught deportment at my school. How about yours?

I remember marching and having to learn how to dance with a girl, and when you were 10 or 11 years of age that was almost a fate worse than death!

The teacher in the photo is Dorothy Chamberlain of Whyalla South Primary School. She would become my mother-in-law some 15 years after this photo was taken.

**1951**

A Broadcast Listeners Licence from 1951. Failure to produce this licence on demand could incur a £50 fine or 6 months imprisonment!

*Courtesy of Michael Brodie*

Up until 1972, radio or TV owners were required to pay for a Broadcast Viewer/Listener Licence. The money collected from the licence fees went to running the operations of the Australian Broadcasting Commission and was finally abolished when it was decided to fund the ABC from general revenue.

Today the ABC costs taxpayers over one billion dollars annually as it grows bigger, opens more channels and has numerous radio stations.

I can never recall paying for a radio listener's licence and I certainly had a transistor from the early 1960s, so I don't believe the licencing fee was enforced in the latter years, but I do recall my mother paying for the licence in the 1950s and remember the vans that would patrol neighbourhoods looking for unlicenced listeners.

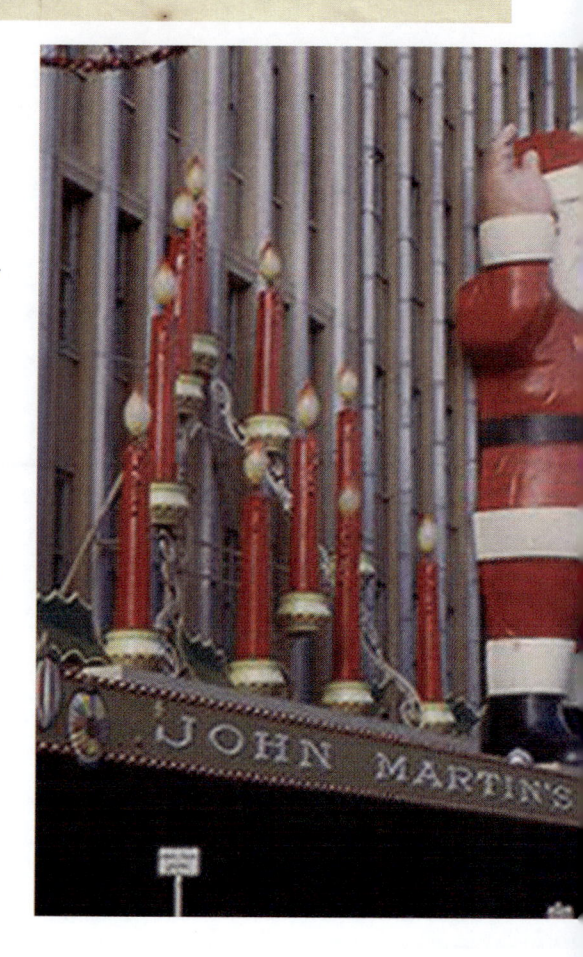

It wasn't Christmas until Johnnies' Christmas Pageant brought Santa to the Magic Cave on the first floor. Everyone who lined up to see Santa got a free Christmas stocking full of goodies: coloured pencils and colouring book, a little roll of Lifesavers and some other lollies, a comic and a few other little treasures and a Santa mask. I remember the stocking had a cardboard backing and a red fishnet material in front. Everyone could take photos too, no charge!

Santa Claus is coming to town. And everybody knew that the *real* Santa was at Johnnies' Magic Cave

*Courtesy of Anthony Harrison*

The much-loved Adelaide columnist and personality Des Colquhoun

*ARW*

Des Colquhoun started at *The Advertiser* in 1948 at the age of 17 as a copy boy and later began a four-year cadetship as a journalist. After stints in Melbourne, London and New York he returned to Adelaide in 1966 as the editorial manager, later becoming general manager of the newspaper. He took on the role of front-page columnist and continued to write his popular column right throughout the 1980s. Des died in 2006.

A survey once found that due to his incisive writing, wit and at times quirky observations of South Australians, Des had become the state's best-known and most admired person.

# 1959

Whereas there used to be many picure theatres in the city (the Regent, Theatre Royal, State, Metro, Wests, Paris, My Fair Lady, Rex, Sturt, Globe, Savoy and the beautiful old Majestic), these days there is only one picture theatre on the city square mile: the Palace Nova.

The Majestic Theatre was 'the most modern theatre in Adelaide during 1916', according to an *Advertiser* report of the day. It was located in King William Street and was adjoined to the Majestic Hotel. It remained as one of Adelaide's leading picture theatres right up until 1967 when it underwent renovations and reopened as the Celebrity Theatre and Restaurant. In 1969 there was another change, this time it became a cinema and live theatre and was renamed The Warner Theatre. It closed at the end of March 1979 and, despite a public petition for heritage listing and protection, the building was demolished in 1981 and a Commonwealth Bank was built on the site.

I recall debate at the time about the irregularity of design going on in the city, which many people saw as a blot on the landscape and loss of history in the city's heart!

I saw a lot of Elvis movies and westerns at the wonderful Majestic Theatre

*State Library of South Australia B17605*

1962

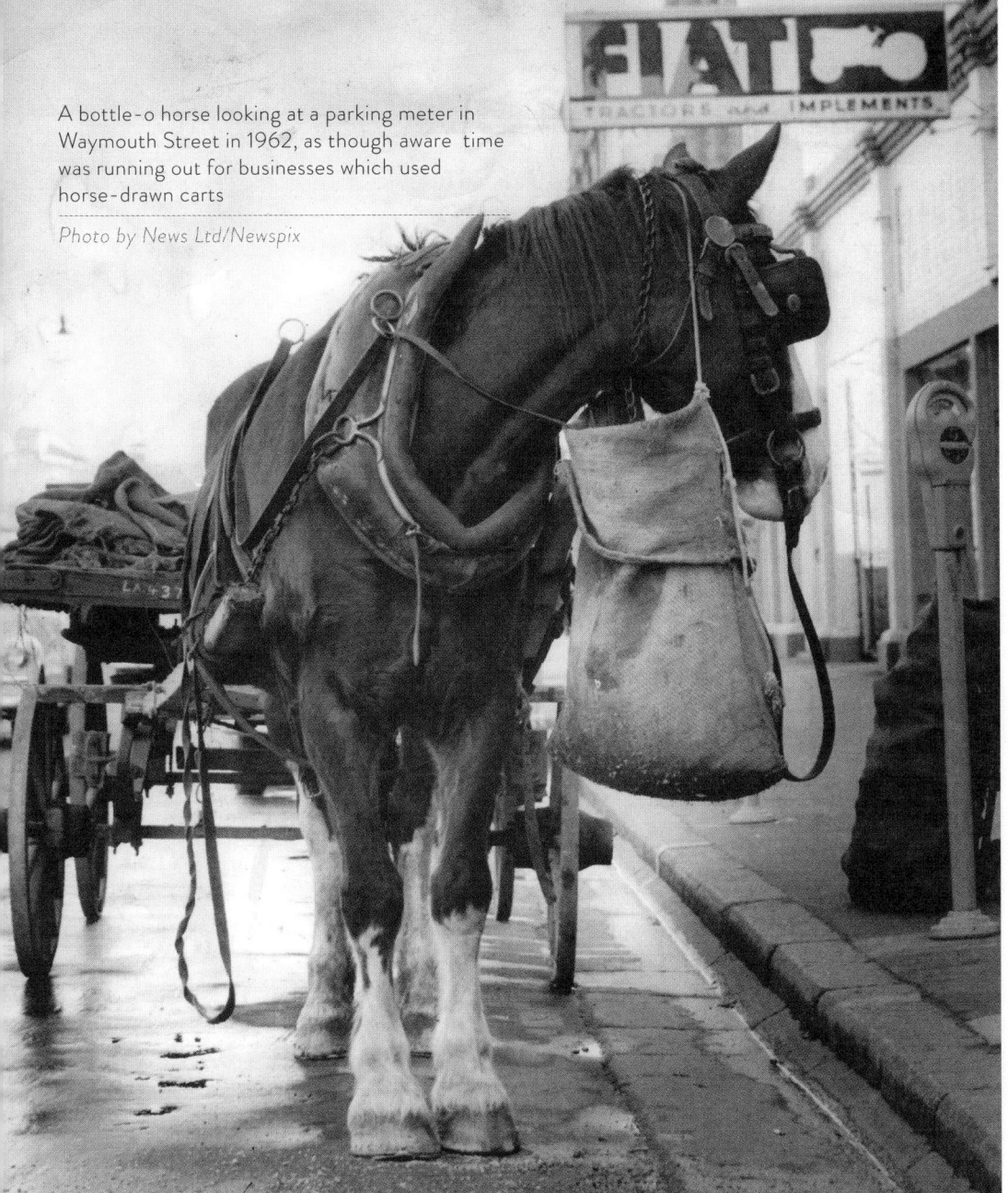

A bottle-o horse looking at a parking meter in Waymouth Street in 1962, as though aware time was running out for businesses which used horse-drawn carts

Photo by News Ltd/Newspix

We've had a photo of the bread being delivered by horse and cart but there was also the bottle-o.

The bottle-o would collect all bottles. Pick-Axe beer bottles were worth almost nothing, something like 4d a dozen, whereas soft-drink bottles were worth 6d for a big one and 3d for a small one. I think standard Coke bottles were 3d.

The bottle-o disappeared sometime during the 1960s giving way to cars, trucks and recycling plants.

1972

Balfour's Tea Rooms in Rundle Street. A favourite place to have lunch in the city when shopping

*Courtesy of San Remo Macaroni Company Pty Ltd*

The name of Balfours has been known to South Australians since 1877 and remains a lunchtime favourite today for delicious pies, pasties, sausage rolls, cakes and buns. Remember being taken to Balfour's Tea Rooms for a treat when shopping or even for lunch? In 1972 the shop was said to be the busiest shop in the southern hemisphere. I know that people still talk about Balfour's Tea Rooms today and tell their children and grandchildren about it. It closed in the late 1980s when the premises were sold.

The shop always had a fresh food smell and it was always crowded – what a wonderful memory!

# #22
## FACT

South Australia food icons:

Villis Pies
Farmer's Union Iced Coffee
Bickfords Brown Lime Cordial
Woodroofe Lemonade
Haigh's Chocolates
Menz Fruchocs
Coopers Pale Ale
Nippy's Orange Juice
Maggie Beer Pheasant Farm Pate, Quince Paste, Verjuice
Coffin Bay Oysters
Southern Rock Lobster
Pie Floaters
(recognised in 2003 as a South Australian Heritage Icon by the National Trust of Australia)
Spring Gully Pickles
St Agnes Brandy
Charlesworth Nuts
Golden North Ice Cream
Kitchener Buns
Bung Fritz

1984

The Milk Carton Regatta, 1984, shows the 'Schimwagon', making slow but steady progress on the Patawalonga at Glenelg

Photo by News Ltd/Newspix

Like the birdman rallies, the milk carton regattas were a fad of the 1980s. Held each year at the Patawalonga from 1980, thousands of people would turn up each year for a full day of fun and laughter. People's imaginations ran wild with some of the crazy craft that took to the water, most sinking without a trace. The first milk carton regatta may have been conducted on the Torrens, but quickly moved to the Pat and was held there for quite a few years.

1958

## 1958

Geoff Cartridge shares his memories of Rundle Street:

Do you remember the crush of pedestrians at the traffic lights before and after work? The buses disgorging hundreds of passengers in the rain. Rundle Street was just packed with cars and pedestrians and buses and rain and humidity! No one could see out of the fogged-up bus windows. And gentlemen would give up their seats for little old ladies and attractive young ones too.

What about lunches at the Hotel Rundle? Three courses for 50 cents! On the corner of King William Street and Hindley Street there was Tunney's Tobacconists with bowls of pipe tobacco displayed in the window. Nearby was a deli where you could buy double cut, ham, salad, asparagus and pineapple rolls for 30 cents. The closest department store was Miller Andersons, which boasted a real tailor, the esteemed Mr Kerrison. The city was really alive then!

How busy was Rundle Street in the late 1950s!

*Photo by News Ltd/Newspix*

# 1886

The spectacular, but now demolished Exhibition Building on North Terrace was built to accommodate the Adelaide Jubilee Exhibition in celebration of the colony's fiftieth birthday in 1887.

The grandeur of the building was a symbol of the colony's progress and booming economy before the recession of the late 19th century set in. The building was much admired and after the exhibition closed it housed numerous associations and events. Some of the more notable were the Art Gallery of South Australia, the South Australian School of Art, the Royal Agricultural and Horticultural Show, and the School of Mines. Through the years it hosted an array of balls, concerts, exhibitions, and events. It even housed circuses and homeless men during the Depression, and was at one stage reinvented as a roller-skating rink, an isolation hospital during the 1918–1920 Spanish flu pandemic, offices, and an examination space.

Gradually its use diminished, especially when the Royal Show was moved to the Wayville Showgrounds in 1925. The building and grounds were vested in the University of Adelaide, but by the late 1950s the building had fallen into disrepair and it was demolished in 1962 to make way for the University of Adelaide's Napier Building and forecourt.

Many people will remember this magnificent building on North Terrace. The Exhibition Building was erected in the 1880s and demolished in 1962 after falling into disrepair

*State Library of South Australia B3105. 1*

1953

# #23
## FACT

Even the referees got caught up in the action of wrestling, trying to give the 'good guys' a bit of a hand against 'the baddies'

*Photo by News Ltd/Newspix*

From the late 1940s and throughout the 1950s, wrestling was a sport that attracted an almost cult-like following in Adelaide. There would be regular events at the Norwood Town Hall, the Tivoli Theatre (later Her Majesty's) in Grote Street and Thebarton Town Hall.

Thousands of fans would roll up to boo 'the baddies' while cheering for the 'good guys'. Skull Murphy, Brute Bernard, Mario Milano, and Killer Karl Kox would have the crowd on its feet. It was all heavily staged of course with the baddies using whatever underhanded tricks they could while the referee's attention was (deliberately) diverted. The good guys always played by the rules, of course.

The FIA Formula One Championship held in Adelaide in 1985 brought Grand Prix Racing to Australia for the first time. In 2014 more than a quarter of a million V8 fans went to the Clipsal 500. The current New Clipsal 500 Lap Record by a V8 Supercar is held by Shane van Gisbergen, driving a Holden Commodore VF.

1948

## 1948

Early on Sunday, 11 April 1948, a vicious storm hit Adelaide with 81 mph winds (130kph) and almost 72mm of rain. The storm was responsible for unroofing houses, bringing down trees and causing enormous damage throughout the city. Beach and coastal areas were particularly affected, with large and small boats wrecked and washed ashore, two ketches destroyed at Outer Harbour, a freighter torn from its moorings at Port Adelaide and, as our photo shows, large sections of the Glenelg Jetty washed away. One man became stranded at the end of the Glenelg Jetty when the mid-section was destroyed by the raging sea and was forced to wait until Monday morning for the seas to abate and the storm to pass, so he could finally be rescued.

The other major incident caused by the storm was the beaching of the survey frigate HMAS *Barcoo*. It was driven ashore at West Beach and attracted large crowds of onlookers until it was finally refloated several days later at high tide.

What was left of the Glenelg jetty after the 1948 storm

*Photo by News Ltd/Newspix*

1886

## 1922

Adelaide's famous frog cakes, first created by Balfours in 1922

*Creative Commons*

The Adelaide Arcade is a really beautiful old building, thank goodness we've still got some left! It was opened in 1885 with 50 shops, each with a showroom downstairs and a workshop upstairs. It was one of the first premises to use the new-fangled electricity and was quite a frontrunner in design and style. It now houses over 100 businesses and is an impressive building, still practical and continues to serve our city well!

One of our city's most beautiful old buildings is the Adelaide Arcade, which first opened in 1885

*State Library of South Australia B2903*

## 1962

Here is the old Mallala track pretty much as I remember it as a teenager. We'd head out with a carload of mates to Mallala on a Saturday (or Sunday) to watch the racing. There wasn't much protective fencing and I can still remember the smell of the exhaust fumes and burning rubber and the traffic jams coming home. It was a great day out!

Davison flashes by in his Cooper Climax at Mallala in 1962

*Photo by News Ltd/Newspix*

Getting your first kitbag was almost like a time-honoured passage into young adulthood. Most boys got their first kitbag when they started high school. Up until then we had a school bag, but going into first year (as it was called back then) we got a new kitbag, all polished and firm.

After a few years the leather would soften and the kitbag would then be quite soft and floppy. My father took his lunch to work every day in his floppy old kitbag, which he must have had for years. Although they got floppy you never needed a new one because they always did the job. I wish I knew where my old kitbag was. Nowadays the backpack has replaced the kitbag.

## 1960

Many Adelaideans gathered for a picnic and a hit of tennis in the The National Park at Belair. It was South Australia's first national park and the second in Australia. During 1896 a kiosk was opened and the first two tennis courts were built. Within twenty years this number had increased to more than forty courts.

The adults would concentrate on the sport and the children would disappear into the bush and play around the creeks and ruins of Old Government House, which was reopened in 1960 to the public.

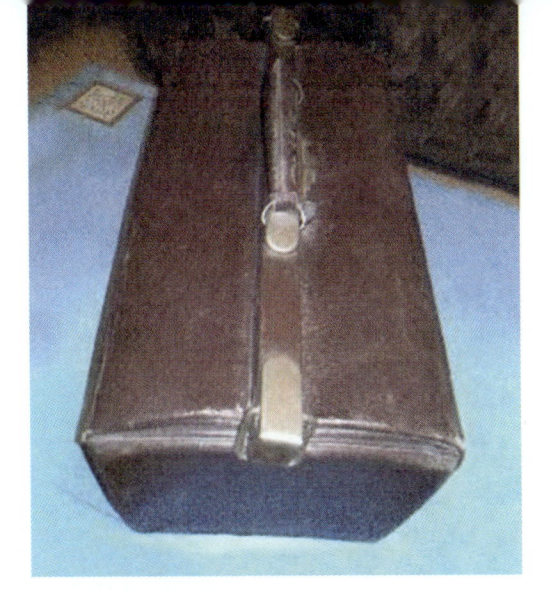

*It fitted perfectly between the old-fashioned handlebars on pushbikes so you could ride to school with your kitbag*

Courtesy of Michael Brodie

*Tennis picnics in The National Park, that kitbag doubled as a picnic hamper, 1960*

Courtesy of Di Quick

Cravens, 1932. Note the policeman on point duty in the days before traffic lights on the corner of Pulteney and Rundle Streets

*State Library of South Australia B6200*

1932

One of Adelaide's big department stores that closed in the early 1970s was Cravens. In the 1950s Adelaide was home to many major South Australian department stores, including Harris Scarfe, John Martins, Peoplestores, Miller Anderson, Cravens, Foy and Gibsons (later Cox Foys), Charles Birks and Charles Moores (Moores on the Square), of which Harris Scarfe is the sole survivor. We now have just the three major department stores in the city: Myers, David Jones and Harris Scarfe. Cravens' site was re-developed as the Centrepoint shopping centre.

1959

Anyone from the 1950s and 1960s will remember the kerosene heater. I recall having to walk to the local service station for some kerosene (which was blue), lugging the drum home, using a hand pump to fill the bottle of the kero heater, tipping it upside down, waiting until the wick was soaked, lighting the wick and putting the round bit on that had the coil which would then heat up and glow red and throw out heat – and an awful lot of fumes too.

Thinking back now I recall that they caused a few fires but I'd say they were probably the cheapest form of heating at the time.

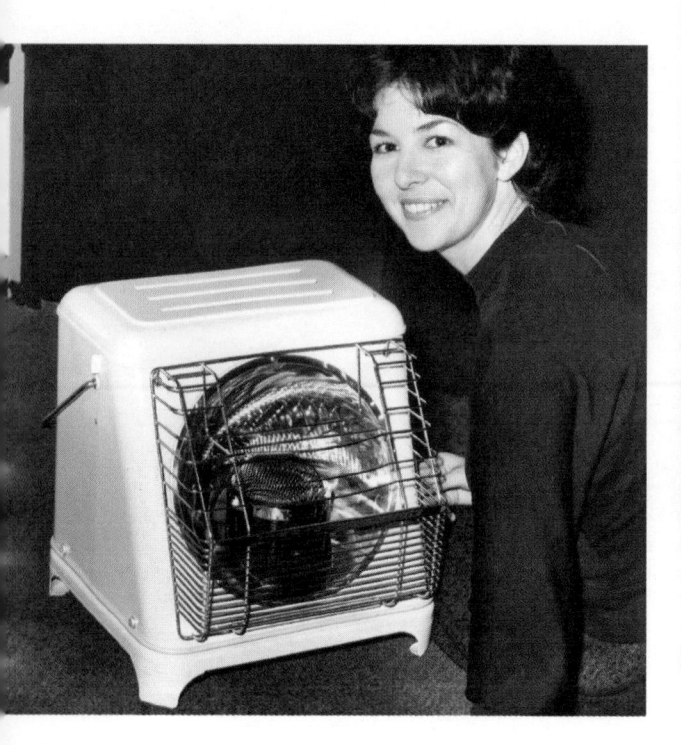

The Fyrside brand kerosene heater was the most popular heater in the 1950s

Photo by John Gusterl/Newspix

# #24
## FACT

Legendary band *The Angels* formed in Adelaide in 1974. Originally called *The Moonshine Jug and String Band*, formed by brothers John and Rick Brewster with their Flinders University friend Doc Neeson, the acoustic blues outfit went on to become one of Australia's legendary rock 'n' roll bands.

1974

The My Fair Lady Theatre in Hindley Street opened in 1966, especially for the Audrey Hepburn film *My Fair Lady*. It was originally owned and operated by Warner Bros and was later taken over by Roadshow Theatre's chain, with the name shortened to Fair Lady Theatre. It was finally taken over by an independent operator and closed in February 1988. It was used briefly for rock concerts, and for a final time in October 1988, when a rock show and disco named 'Farewell to a Fair Lady' was held in the building. The Fair Lady Theatre was demolished in late 1989. A small shopping mall was built on the site, which included a five-screen Greater Union Hindley Street cinema, located at the rear. That has now also closed.

The Fair Lady Theatre in Hindley Street in 1974 featuring Jon Voight in *The Odessa File*

*State Library of South Australia B29905*
*Ronald Praite, coutesy of John Praite*

# 1954

On 1 March 1954 at 3.40am, Adelaide experienced its last big earthquake. It had a reported magnitude of 5.6 on the Richter Scale and damaged buildings across the city. Heavy tremors, some lasting up to 30 seconds, shook half the state from an epicentre near Darlington. Only three people were reported injured and the total cost of damage was estimated at around £17 million (about $500 million in today's money). Most people slept through it, but there was some serious damage done to buildings, including this shoe shop in Franklin Street in the city.

Adelaide experiences minor earthquakes occasionally. Were you in town for the last big earthquake in 1954?

*Photo by News Ltd/Newspix*

# 1965

The opening line-up of personalities on SAS 10 in 1965, (from left) Gail Spiro, Roger Cardwell, Michele Kenny, Noel O'Connor and Paul Griffiths

*Courtesy of Noel O'Connor*

Channel 10, Adelaide's third commercial TV station, commenced broadcasting on 26 July 1965. Until then Adelaide had been served by just two commercial channels (9 and 7, broadcasting since 1959) and, since 1960, the non-commercial ABC, Channel 2. Some of the personalities and characters from those early years included Roger Cardwell, Noel O'Connor and Jane Reilly along with children's favourites: Bobo the Clown and Fat Cat.

Shows introduced to Adelaide audiences by the new channel included *Romper Room*, *Crackerjack*, *The Early Birds* and *Fat Cat and Friends*. Music programs like *New Faces* and *Pot Luck*, *Trax* and *In Time* attracted big local audiences. Many people will recall *Touch of Elegance* and the Friday night movie marathons with Deadly Earnest played by Hedley Cullen. From 1973 to 1989 Channel 10 gave us the *Christmas Appeal Telethon* hosted by Gary Meadows. It was magical local entertainment for a wonderful cause.

In a rather bizarre event in 1987, SAS 10 and ADS 7 swapped call signs. It appears that, as the TV industry was consolidating throughout Australia, the two channels had become associated with different ownership groups and it was decided the simplest solution to the problem was to simply exchange call signs. We all went to bed one night watching Channel 10 and when we woke up in the morning the very same channel was calling itself Channel 7.

1957

## 1957

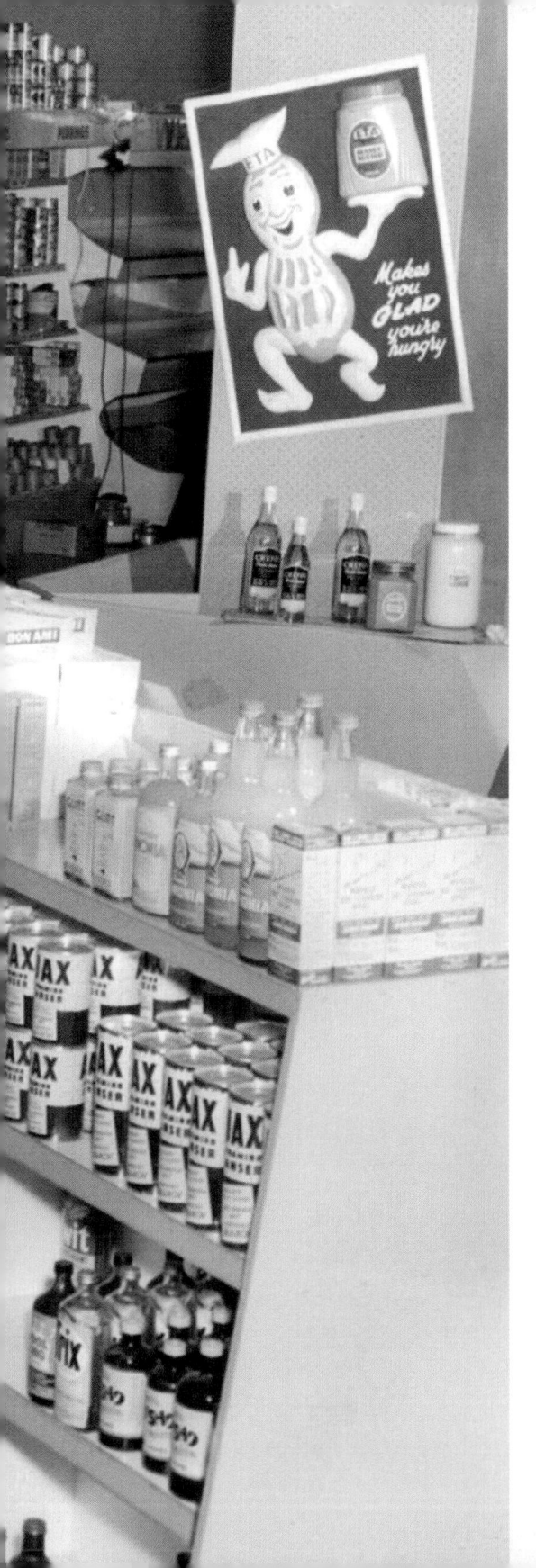

Before the large chain supermarkets of Coles and Woolies and the mega shopping centres, most Adelaideans in the 1950s and '60s picked up essential daily items from the corner shop.

The local little independent shop, Serv-Wel or 4 Square Stores stocked everything from milk and bread to shoe polish, flour, sugar, fruit and veg, newspapers and even cigarettes. The local corner shop, or deli, was the centre of many communities, as well as a source of income for the families who ran them, many of them immigrants, who brought their trading skills with them from Greece and Italy.

There were also specialist greengrocers with a truck or bus, a shop on wheels, that would do a regular round two or three times a week and deliver fresh fruit and veg around the suburbs.

*A little of almost everything. The Unley grocery store/supermarket in 1957*

Photo by News Ltd/Newspix

# 1965

Photos of the city area in the 1960s bring back so many memories to us local boomers. Rundle Street in those years was the shopping precinct as there were no big suburban shopping centres back then. Car fanatics will have a ball with this, look at some of those great old cars!!

Rundle Street looking west in 1965, before it became a pedestrian mall

*Photo by Phil Lambourne /Newspix*

1984

In June 1984 Boy George arrived in Adelaide for a personal appearance. From left Greg Clark, Jon Moss, Mikey Craig, John Bannon, Boy George, Ian Molly Meldrum and Roy Hay

*Courtesy of Greg Clark and 5AD*

Greg Clark (formerly of Radio 5AD) shared some memories of 'A big big day for the radio station. 25,000 people in Rundle Mall, the world's hottest group in town. All the big names are there on the old Richmond overpass (now demolished) – Unforgettable'!

It was an amazing day. Even though I was working at a rival radio station (5DN), we went along and were amazed at the huge crowd. Nothing like the 300,000 who turned out for the Beatles twenty years earlier of course, but it was a very exciting and memorable event.

## 1958

The Koala Farm, complete with its camels, ponies, snakes, seals and, of course, koalas, was a feature in the 1950s, until 1960. It caused a bit of a stir when it was first set up because it was a commercial venture and was the first commercial venture on the Parklands.

Barbara Hann recalls 'Lewis, my brother and I became very familiar with the farm back in those days. Although small, I still remember the fun we had at the Farm ... I remember being taken by my father on many occasions, whilst my parents visited my sister, Alison, in hospital [Adelaide Children's Hospital]'.

Professor Julius Sumner Miller with Alistair McHarg, entertainer, compere and a mean piano player
*Courtesy of Noel O'Connor*

*Why is it so?* Was the ground-breaking TV series with the enigmatic Professor Julius Sumner Miller. It ran on the ABC from 1963 to 1986. Professor Miller's infectious enthusiasm for physics delighted, educated and entertained generations of Australians, most of whom have at some point asked each other 'Why is it so?' in the characteristic Julius Sumner Miller voice!

### 1969

The City Baths were demolished the year this photo was taken, 1969, to make way for the Festival Centre complex after the Adelaide Swimming Centre (now Adelaide Aquatic Centre) was opened in the northern Parklands.

Photographer Frank Hall used to go to buildings and sites that had been earmarked for demolition around the city and take a photographic record. Thankfully Frank and his wife Elaine have shared many of their priceless photos with us at 'Adelaide Remember When'.

Dale Barry, Robyn Whitehead and Sue Cameron enjoy a close encounter with a koala and its baby at the Koala Farm in 1958
*Photo by Dick Joyner/Newspix*

Taken from the back of the Adelaide Railway Station, looking towards the City Baths, in 1969
*Frank Hall, courtesy of Elaine Hall*

1976

# #25
## FACT

Gavin Wanganeen played junior football for the Salisbury North Hawks and attended Salisbury East High School, in 1993 becoming the first Aboriginal AFL player to become a Brownlow medallist. He was Port Adelaide Power's inaugural captain and played for the team from 1997 to 2006, the first Indigenous footballer to play 300 games.

There are many stories about George who was the Adelaide Zoo orang-utan. He loved his footy and his old hessian bag

*Photo by Barry O'Brien/Newspix*

George was an orang-utan who delighted crowds for decades with his antics. I recall being at the zoo with my mother and sisters and George was busy throwing poo at everyone outside his cage. There are many stories and legends about George.

Apparently one night he escaped from his enclosure and climbed up a tree within the zoo grounds. Hoogen, his keeper at the time, had to go into the zoo to talk him down. George climbed down the tree and hand-in-hand walked back in to his cage.

George died in 1976 and his bones are housed in the old elephant house, now the 'Elephant Interpretation Centre'.

1940

Bill Flett and Ruby delivering milk to Mount Gambier residents in the late 1940s

*State Library of South Australia B69699*

During the 1940s and '50s, milk was scooped from large milk cans into billies left out the front of the house. It was usually delivered by horse and cart, and the horse knew the delivery route, when to stop and when to go again. Most of Adelaide's milk supply at that time was processed by Amscol, the Adelaide Milk Supply Co-Operative. Milk bottles were introduced mid century.

I always feel that the milk was thicker then, and there was cream on the top. And mum used to 'scald' the milk which gave it a skin that we used to have with bread and jam.

# 1972

Back before the world was fully air-conditioned, and on really hot Adelaide summer days, kids would wait for Dad to get home and then pester the parents to take them to the beach. Sometimes (provided homework was done) it worked for me and there'd be a cool breeze at the beach and we'd stay until maybe 9 o'clock and then go home to a stinking hot house with not even an electric fan in those times. We were never allowed to jump off the jetty, but I remember lots of kids leaping off without a care in the world. Great memories. Notice the old sideshows and merry-go-round on the foreshore.

Glenelg Jetty jumping, 1972

*City of Holdfast Bay Collection*

1972

## 1939

One of the great discussions we have in Adelaide is about the weather, especially when it starts to heat up in summer or get chilly in winter.

Peter Goers from ABC Radio wrote a piece in his *Sunday Mail* column last summer, which typifies how most Adelaideans feel about the hot summers and the present-day reaction to a bit of heat:

> It'd be a 110 degrees in the shade and my grandparents would be sweltering, drinking hot tea and looking at the air-conditioner turned off. 'Don't worry about us. We'll be all right. It was hotter in Perth. We're not made of money …'.
>
> We were tougher then. We were toughened by tin roofs, sleep-outs and lean-tos. We were told: 'Horses sweat, men perspire and women glow.'
>
> As kiddies we gambolled under the sprinkler on the buffalo-grass back lawn in our cotton tops. Laughing. And the dog joined in. We'd go to the beach and pool with our Dickies towels, zinc-creamed noses and strawberry Snip moustache.
>
> We'd sleep out on the front lawn after watching the TV that had been dragged out on to the front veranda. You wouldn't do that now on a bit of plastic lawn next to the feature garage. More's the pity.

Fritz Goers, Peter's uncle: 'the pavement back then was so hot you could fry an egg on it!'

*Photo by News Ltd/Newspix*

Kenny Peplow and his sister off to the local Sunday School in the 1950s dressed in their Sunday best

*Courtesy of Kenny Peplow*

Religion played a much bigger role in the community as we were growing up from the 1950s to the late 1970s. Every Sunday most people in our neighbourhood would dress in their best clothes and attend a local church. There were special outings and events organised just for the kiddies while parents attended service.

As Catholics we never had a Sunday School as such, but dressed every Sunday in our best and went off to Mass.

1952

# #26
FACT

Did you know that the painter Jeffrey Smart, the former Prime Minister Julia Gillard, former premier John Bannon, former governor Sir Mark Oliphant and former Australian of the Year Lowitja O'Donoghue all attended Unley High School in Netherby?

# 1972

In 2003, the pie floater was recognised as a South Australian Heritage Icon by the National Trust of Australia. Many were served outside the GPO, as pictured here

*Photo by Sarah Reed/Newspix*

The Norwood Pie Cart, 1972, located on The Parade, adjacent to the Norwood Town Hall

*Photo by News Ltd/Newspix*

Adelaide once had a love affair with pie carts. The first one opened in 1860, on the corner of Franklin Street and King William Street outside the GPO, and by the end of the 1900s there were thirteen dotted around the city. By 1915, the number had been gradually reduced to nine. As eating habits changed, there were just two left by 1958: Cowley's Pie Cart on the corner of Franklin and King William Streets, outside the GPO; and the Balfour's Pie Cart, in front of the Railway Station on North Terrace.

Talk about icons! The GPO pie cart has been officially recognised as the longest-running food outlet in South Australia by the National Trust and the pie floater has been declared a national icon! Sadly there are no pie carts left in Adelaide now. The Railway Station Pie Cart in North Terrace was forced to close in 2007 while extensions were being completed to the tramline in North Terrace and never reopened; and the GPO Pie Cart was closed in October 2010.

The Norwood Pie Cart lasted for more than 80 years on the Parade. It was also the only place where members of the public could buy draft Hall's 'Stonie' ginger beer directly from the keg.

## 1965

Once upon a time as you approached Glenelg beach along Anzac Highway you could see the water. Glenelg was our most popular beach with sideshows, long stretches of soft white sand and always a safe swimming environment. Most of that Glenelg disappeared once the major developers moved in and it's turned into an area for large apartment buildings, hotels and other up-market establishments. Yes, it's still Glenelg but iconic old areas and the view have disappeared and it's just not the beach we knew and loved in our youth!

The days of surf, sun and sand. Glenelg beach back in 1965

*Courtesy of Glenelg Surf Lifesaving Club*

# 1976

John Nash was a house painter and an amateur clairvoyant who predicted that Adelaide would be destroyed by an earthquake and tidal wave at noon on 19 January 1976. Hundreds of people fled inland as far as the Riverland, their cars loaded with all their possessions, to avoid the tsunami. The story got major press coverage with BBC London even sending out a TV crew. Premier Don Dunstan made international headlines by going to Glenelg beach to reassure everyone that there was no danger. About 2000 people also turned up at the beach and at midday there was a countdown, but nothing happened. Bit of a fizzer really.

Premier Don Dunstan defies doomsayer John Nash's prediction and joins crowds at Glenelg Beach

*Photo by News Ltd/Newspix*

# #27
## FACT

Redgum's 'I was only 19', an emotional song with powerful lyrics about a Vietnam veteran, is one of the best-known popular songs in Australia. Released in 1980, it was written by John Schumann, a former Marion High School teacher.

When I was at school we ordered from the school tuck shop, writing our order on a plain paper bag. When my children went to school in the 1970s and '80s they would fill out one of these brown paper bags for lunch orders and then the lunch monitor would take them to the school canteen so they could get it brought back to the classroom for lunch.

The canteen would be staffed by volunteer parents and they'd make sure the kids got their lunch bags filled with whatever they wanted. The children who were the lunch monitors would come in just before lunch to pick them up and they'd all be happily chatting away while they waited for the lunch ladies to get their class's lunch box for them.

Who remembers being Lunch Monitor? I'll have a Balfour's pie with sauce and a Kitchener bun please!

*Courtesy of Detpak Packaging*

1975

1951

'Men Swear by Thwaites for Men's Wear'
*State Library of South Australia. PRG 287/1/15/90*

1951

'Thwaites Corner' was on the south-west corner of Rundle and Pulteney Streets all through our growing up years.

There's a Telstra shop on that corner these days, and Rundle Street is now Rundle Mall, but here's a photo from 1951, looking west from the corner of Rundle Street and Pulteney Street. Coles and National Bank can be seen along the northern side of Rundle Street.

## 1961

On Friday, 11 March 1960, Adelaide got its third TV station with the opening of the ABC's channel, ABS 2. Kay Withers was the first female announcer and news presenter, also appearing on camera each night and previewing the evening's line-up of shows. Other well-known presenters in those early years, included Bob Caldicott, Clive Hale, Bob Moore and Alan Hodgson.

ABS Channel 2 presenter Kay Withers broke new ground on Adelaide TV in the early 1960s

*Courtesy of Keith Birks*

An Easter tradition in Adelaide. A picnic from the boot of the car in the centre of Oakbank Racecourse. This photo is from 1957

*Photo by News Ltd/Newspix*

1957

There are many traditions in Adelaide. Every year thousands of people head to the Adelaide Hills for the annual Easter Picnic Race Meeting at Oakbank. For many the real tradition is to park in the centre of the track, open the car boot and lay out a picnic on the grass. Many picnickers will not watch one race during the entire day of racing, instead enjoying the company of their family or friends and other picnickers nearby.

1947

AMSCOL stands for Adelaide Milk Supply Co-Operative Limited and the factory was situated in Carrington Street. Amscol opened in 1922 and was mainly responsible for the supply of bottled milk to the city and suburbs, but it also produced cream, cheese, ice-cream and butter. Classic products included the original 'brick' of ice-cream in a waxed cardboard box, Berry Bars and the small tub of ice-cream called the Dandy. Amscol was eventually taken over by Streets in the early 1980s and the old Amscol building was demolished.

1985

Lots to do for young and old at Downtown

*Photo by Graham Tidy/Newspix*

Downtown first opened at 65 Hindley Street in the late 1970s as a new multi-faceted complex with roller-skating, dodgem cars, sideshows, arcade games, a shooting gallery and a restaurant. In those days parents would take the kids for a night out at Downtown, where they could have a meal in the restaurant and let the kids have the time of their lives roller-skating or playing the arcade games.

In the mid 1980s Downtown was relocated down the road towards King William Street in an old classic cinema building (which even today has the old Downtown sign out the front). The new facility was much smaller, and from memory the restaurant disappeared. As time went on Hindley Street became a no-go zone for families and Downtown finally closed in the late 1980s. The original Downtown building at 65 Hindley was torn down and replaced by a brand new hotel that we now know as the Holiday Inn.

'It's a food, not a fad.' Adelaideans will tell you that Amscol produced the best ice-cream ever made!

*State Library of South Australia B54942*

233

# 1990

TV and radio personality and former beach girl, Jane Reilly

*Photo by Sarah Reed/Newspix*

The Festival of Arts display, 1970

*Courtesy of Anthony Harrison*

Jane Reilly has been a familiar face on TV and a familiar voice on radio for as long as I can remember. Jane was Miss Australia Beach Girl in 1974 and from there branched out into the media hosting children's programs with Fat Cat, followed by several stints on radio, then back to TV as Channel Ten News weather presenter and currently back on radio as a high-profile news and talk presenter on the breakfast program at 5AA.

Jane's contribution and dedication to her work in the media has won her a host of awards and accolades including the prestigious MBF national media award, two years running, and in 1995, she was named a Family Ambassador for the Office of Families.

1970

The banks at the back of the West End Brewery are best known for the annual Christmas display. Every year thousands of people take their children and grandchildren to view the display that has been an Adelaide favourite for many years.

How many remember that the Brewery also used to put on a riverbank display at Easter and every second year for the Adelaide Festival of Arts?

With the Festival now an annual event, many of our page followers thought it would be a great idea to see the Christmas display extended to now take in the Festival and then Easter.

Easter Riverbank Display, West End Brewery, 1967

*Courtesy of Anthony Harrison*

1967

# 1967

Adelaide is very proud of its Central Market. The history of the market goes back to 1869, when on Saturday, 23 January, at 3.15am a group of market gardeners made their way to a site between Gouger and Grote Streets and started to sell their produce.

Over 500 people attended that first market day and all stock was sold out by 6am! The Central Market as we know it today really started in 1965 with a big redevelopment program that was completed along with a new rooftop car park in June 1966.

Adelaide's Central Market in 1967. It is our most visited tourist attraction

*State Library of South Australia B22053*

## 2011

The Adelaide Oval has undergone a major upgrade and is now the home of AFL football. While it was sad to lose such a pretty cricket ground, the new stadium offers all modern amenities and it's certainly a huge improvement on the old Footy Park at West Lakes. At the 'cathedral end' was the old scoreboard and the spires of St Peter's Cathedral behind the Moreton Bay fig trees. At the 100th birthday celebration of the scoreboard, back in 2011, SACA president Ian McLachlan said, 'Being the only operational scoreboard of its type in the Southern hemisphere, the scoreboard is arguably one of the best in the world in that it tells the whole story of the game at any one point.'

1970

Growing up listening to cricket commentators from all over the globe, it was not at all uncommon to hear them describing the beauty of the Adelaide cricket ground, falling into raptures about the colour and the view over the 'cathedral end' at the 'world's prettiest cricket ground'

*Photo by News Ltd/Newspix (Adelaide Now)*

Triple Magarey Medallist Lindsay Head charging out onto the ground for a record 327th, and his last game for West Torrens against Norwood in 1970

*Photo by News Ltd/Newspix*

West Torrens Football Club was an Australian Rules football club that competed in the SANFL from 1897 to 1990. In 1991, the club was merged with neighbouring Woodville Football Club to form the Woodville–West Torrens Eagles.

## 1965

It seemed every former cinema in suburban Adelaide was home to the iconic Tom the Cheap supermarkets. I suppose Tom helped protect buildings and stopped them from being demolished. Before IGA, Tom competed against Serv-Wel, 4 Square, Big Heart and Foodland. Did you shop there? Or work there?

'Tom' was Tom Wardle, a popular Lord Mayor of Perth from 1967 to 1972. He started his discount grocery business with one store in Perth in 1956 after a visit to Europe where he noticed the trend was away from serving behind a counter to self-service shopping. He opened his first 'Tom the Cheap' in Adelaide in 1961 and by 1965 had 24 stores throughout South Australia. The company collapsed financially in 1978.

Almost everybody in Adelaide recalls Tom the Cheap
Photo by News Ltd/Newspix

Ernie Sigley performing a song with local band The Viscounts: John Michell, David Seymour-Smith and Lew Tamblyn. From the scrapbooks of John Michell
State Library of South Australia PRG 1547

## 1970

Ernie Sigley had started out as a turntable operator back in 1952 on Radio 3DB in Melbourne and in 1957 got his first break into TV as the host of *Teenage Mailbag* on Channel 7. He then worked in London radio for about three years before returning to Australia and in the early 1960s acted as compere of *Adelaide Tonight*.

Ernie's larrikin style earned him a large following and he was one of our most popular TV personalities until he returned to Melbourne in 1973 to replace Graham Kennedy on *In Melbourne Tonight*. He went to air each night totally unscripted and unrehearsed, which often landed him in hot water. Yet that approach seemed to endear him to viewers since he and co-host Anne Wills scored a swag of Logie awards for most popular personalities in South Australia.

When we went to the local butcher shop, Mum would ask for hoggitt (don't think we could afford lamb) and sausages, and the butcher would cut off a generous slice of fritz or a bit of raw sausage for us kids, standing waiting patiently, making swirly patterns in the sawdust on the floor.

The butcher always had his knife sharpener at the ready or a machete on his big chopping block and an electric saw to cut the joints while you were there in the shop. He wrapped things like liver, kidneys and hearts in butchers' white paper, which we could have for drawing on later, if it wasn't too messy. So different to the sanitised sparkling butcher shops of today, or the meat section of supermarkets where everything is pre-wrapped in plastic.

Michael Brodie's local 'family butcher' in Murray Street, Lower Mitcham/Clapham is now a private dwelling

*Courtesy of Michael Brodie*

1970

Who remembers Bob Francis as the compere of the Princeton Club, the Hi Fi Club and his radio program *The Sunset Show* on 5AD in the early 1960s? He was one of Adelaide's first real DJs and also the main instigator of getting the Beatles here in 1964 with 80,000 signatures on a petition. He was also one of the earliest exponents of talk radio when he joined up with Andy Thorpe in the late 1960s and then went on to manage 5AD in the halcyon days of Baz and Pilko. He finished his career back on air as a night-time talk host, but as usual it was no ordinary show. Bob became Adelaide's own 'shock jock', outspoken, irreverent, unafraid to take on anyone or discuss anything. Bob has recently retired after some 57 years in the entertainment industry.

Bob Francis, from his Radio 5AD days in 1970

*News Ltd Photos, Herald Sun*

# #28
## FACT

Adelaide is the driest of Australia's capital cities. Its coldest recorded temperature was 0.4° on 16 July 1982. The hottest temperature recorded was 46.1 °C on 12 January 1939, but summer 2013–14 broke records for the greatest number of days exceeding 35°.

### 1969

The Apollo Stadium, home to some serious rock concerts and some of the biggest musical acts in the world from the 1970s to 1991

*Photo by Ian Coventry/Newspix*

Apollo Stadium in Richmond was the main venue for rock concerts in its day, but was first and foremost a basketball stadium. It opened in 1969 and was named Apollo after the moon landing of that same year. Up until then Centennial Hall had been the main venue for concerts, but Apollo Stadium could seat almost 4000 people and thus became the scene for some of the most exciting acts of the 1970s and '80s including Queen, AC/DC, Cold Chisel, U2, Ike & Tina Turner, INXS and Beach Boys. In 1991 the Adelaide Entertainment Centre was built with seating for 12,000 and in 1992 the new home of basketball, The Clipsal Powerhouse, was opened. Apollo Stadium then became a church for a while, but was eventually sold and demolished and the area was redeveloped for housing.

# 1977

The original Coles had a cafeteria on the first floor. Coles was not a supermarket in those days, more like a '$2 shop' and my wife remembers shopping there as a child for pop beads and rings.

I'm sure many will remember having lunch in the cafeteria with mum, while on a shopping expedition.

Coles in Rundle Mall in 1977. Remember the cafeteria on the first floor?

*State Library of South Australia B35076*

## 1987

In the ongoing debate about the destruction of heritage buildings in Adelaide, the old House of Chow looms large. I'm talking of course about the original building on the opposite side of Hutt Street to the present restaurant structure.

In late 1987 the Adelaide City Council approved an application to demolish the old House of Chow and replace it with a three-storey office building. The City Planner observed at the time that there had been extensive renovations both inside and outside the building and as there was no heritage listing, the building could be demolished. Many people did not agree with his decision however and even within the ACC there was much heated debate about valuable heritage buildings being destroyed and replaced with bland and boring structures. The debate about the building's future raged for several years and after a time the State Government got involved and the ACC finally voted in 1991 against the demolition. However by then the House of Chow had been damaged beyond repair and a union ban was eventually placed on the site because non-union labour had been used in the demolition work, which had already commenced. The site remained vacant for many years.

The original House of Chow in Hutt Street was a beautiful and grand building, built in 1870, but more than 100 years later had no heritage listing

*State Library of South Australia B53935*

# 1948

On 2 March 1948 Charles Moore's department store in Victoria Square was reduced to a shell by a fire that broke out at about 6.30pm, raged for about three and a half hours and caused an estimated £500,000 damage. It was a most spectacular fire with flames leaping 20 feet high through the roof before it collapsed. By morning the building, erected in 1916, was a scene of devastation, although amazingly the marble staircase, a well-known feature of the store, survived relatively unscathed. No-one died in the inferno, although several fire fighters were injured. The store was rebuilt and continued trading as Charles Moore's until 1980 when the business closed down. The State Government bought the building and turned it into law courts, now known as the Sir Samuel Way Building.

One of Adelaide's most famous fires completely destroyed Moore's Department Store in Victoria Square in 1948

*State Library of South Australia B21599*

1983

# #29
## FACT

*Max Schubert with his famous Grange Hermitage wine*
Photo by News Ltd/Newspix

The thing I remember most about Max Schubert was his incredible humility. He was feted around the world as the finest wine-maker of his day but remained unaffected by the honours and compliments that were heaped on him.

Max had joined Penfolds in the early 1930s as a messenger boy and became chief winemaker in 1948. His 1955 vintage of Grange Hermitage was submitted to wine competitions, beginning in 1962 and over the years has won more than 50 gold medals. The 1971 vintage won first prize in the Wine Olympics in Paris while the 1990 vintage was named 'Red Wine of the Year' by *Wine Spectator* magazine in 1995.

Max received many awards, including Member of the Order of Australia (AM) and the inaugural Maurice O'Shea Award for his contribution to the Australian wine industry. He was included in the *Sydney Morning Herald*'s 100 most influential Australians of the 20th century, which was published in 2001. Max died in 1994.

With Colin Thiele's *Storm Boy* and Mem Fox's *Possum Magic*, Adelaide authors have given children some of the most-loved books in Australia, not to mention the beloved animal characters Mr Percival and Hush. *Storm Boy* has never been out of print since it was published in 1963 and *Possum Magic*, published 30 years ago, is Australia's best-selling children's picture book.

# 2008

Adelaide was in mourning after the death of its 83-year-old Greater Flamingo in 2013. Affectionately known as 'Greater', the bird was a favourite among zoo-goers for generations.

Greater was the world's oldest flamingo and the last Greater Flamingo to have resided in Australia. It had arrived at Adelaide Zoo back in the 1930s. The flamingo exhibit was opened in 1885, and is one of the few exhibits to have remained in the same position to date. Originally it was stocked with 10 flamingos, however most died during the drought of 1915.

Greater remained strong to the end, even surviving a vicious attack by three teenagers in 2008, which shocked animal lovers around the world.

Greater the Flamingo at Adelaide Zoo

*Creative Commons*

Friends and relatives of Darwin residents, queue at Red Cross House in Adelaide awaiting information about their loved ones on Boxing Day, 1974

*Photo by News Ltd/Newspix*

1974

Adelaide played a major role in helping survivors of one of Australia's most devastating storms: Cyclone Tracy.

Tracy killed 65 people and destroyed more than 70% of Darwin's buildings and infrastructure when she struck on Christmas Eve, 1974. In the days that followed more than 30,000 people were evacuated, including 6000 who were flown direct to Adelaide where they were met by friends and family, while thousands more crowded the highways and drove south seeking refuge in Adelaide.

# 1958

Trams first appeared in Adelaide in the 1870s. By 1900 there were eight privately owned horse tram companies providing a public transport system, running on 74 miles of track serving Adelaide's population of 162,000. At its peak in 1945, the tramways carried passengers on 95 million trips, but by 1951 patronage began to decline, mainly due to the lifting of wartime petrol rationing and the rising ownership of the family car. Over the next seven years it was decided to replace trams with electric trolley buses and the last tram made the run to Cheltenham on 22 November 1958. Fortunately for Adelaide, the Glenelg tramline escaped the recommended closure and was allowed to continue until eventually stirring the revival of a new tramway system.

All aboard for the last tram to St Peters. Passengers crowd on board the last city tram in 1958

*Photo by News Ltd/Newspix*

1982

Hilton workers and builders celebrate the completion of the building in October 1982, just prior to its opening

*Photo by News Ltd/Newspix*

Adelaide got its first five-star international hotel in 1982! Yep, we had a long wait. There was much excitement when it was announced that the Hilton was coming to Adelaide and at the same time there were to be international flights into Adelaide with an international air terminal.

It cost $44 million to complete and right through the 1980s and into the '90s was always quite the place to be. I must admit I haven't been to the Hilton in a while now, but I enjoyed some of the great concerts there back in the 1980s, including Sammy Davis Jr, Andy Williams and Peter Allen.

There are many stories about the South Australian Hotel which stood on North Terrace for almost 100 years. Legend has it that the head waiter at the hotel, Louis (Lewy) Cotton, who had held the position for 51 years until the hotel was demolished in 1971, reigned supreme in the dining room and enforced a strict dress code.

He would fearlessly banish anyone from the dining room who did not conform with the rigorous code. He once refused the Queen's dressmaker admittance and dismissed radio superstar and quizmaster Bob Dyer for wearing a polka-dot cravat. 'Have we a tie, sir?' Louis inquired of Dyer. 'We might have – but I haven't,' quipped Dyer. And so the star named as the 'best-dressed man in Australian entertainment' only a year before was politely, yet firmly, shown the door.

We need a Louis or two now, don't you think?

*The grand staircase of the South Australian Hotel*
State Library of South Australia B40806

**1982**

Lots of fun to be had inside this rather ugly exterior that was likened to a 'giant dog dropping'
*Photo by David Cronin/Newspix*

Magic Mountain was a theme park in Glenelg that opened in December 1982. The four water slides (the largest in the southern hemisphere at the time) were very popular during the hot Adelaide summers. Other attractions included the historic carousel, mini-golf, bumper boats, dodgem cars and sky cycles, pinball machines, a shooting gallery and arcade games.

The Magic Mountain was eventually demolished amid some controversy late in 2004 as part of the final stage of the Holdfast Shores development and replaced by The Beach House in 2006.

1957

Looking west along Rundle Street with Myers in the foreground, you can see how busy, if not chaotic, the heart of the city could be at Christmas time. Note the decorations on Myers. Near the top of the photo is a throng of pedestrians crossing King William Street. The 'Royal' sign must be outside the old Theatre Royal in Hindley Street.

# 1985

KG Cunningham. Without doubt, the most passionate sports broadcaster in Adelaide

*State Library of South Australia B72636/171 Messenger Press photo*

If you love sport and you live in Adelaide, you can't help but know KG. Following a sporting career as a state cricketer and SANFL umpire, KG Cunningham became a TV and radio sports presenter. He ran the first regular 'all-sports' radio drive-time program in Australia on 5DN from 1977 until 1991, when he changed to Radio 5AA.

During the 1980s KG hosted his own 30-minute football show on Channel 9, *KG's Footy Show* and was also the weekend sports presenter for Channel 9 news over 20 years until he joined Channel 7 in 2005.

KG has always been a passionate South Australian and that can lead him to make sometimes controversial statements, but he is much admired for his passion and unwavering stand for the betterment of sport in this state.

Christmas rush, 1957, in Rundle Street. Maybe we see here one of the reasons they decided to turn this stretch of the city into a mall?

*Photo by Dick Joyner/Newspix*

A NewSouth book

*Published by*
NewSouth Publishing
University of New South Wales Press Ltd
University of New South Wales
Sydney NSW 2052
AUSTRALIA
newsouthpublishing.com

© Bob Byrne 2014
First published 2014

10 9 8 7 6 5 4 3 2

This book is copyright. Apart from any fair dealing for the purpose of private study, research, criticism or review, as permitted under the Copyright Act, no part may be reproduced by any process without written permission. Inquiries should be addressed to the publisher.

National Library of Australia
Cataloguing-in-Publication entry
Author: Byrne, Bob, author.
Title: Adelaide remember when/Bob Byrne.
ISBN: 9781742232201 (paperback)
Subjects: Adelaide (S. Aust.) – History.
Adelaide (S. Aust.) – Social life and customs.
Dewey Number: 994.231

DESIGN Di Quick
FRONT COVER Children at Ethelton Primary School drinking 'school milk' in 1960. Photo courtesy of Lynda Vaughan, shows her sister Dallas McDonald (née Wellington) second from right, with her classmates. Ethelton Primary was closed when the school was amalgamated with Semaphore Primary; A hive of activity at the City Baths on a hot Adelaide summer's day in the 1950s. Photo by Bill Krischock/Newspix
BACK COVER School sports day. Photo by News Ltd/Newspix; Dazzleland amusement park at the REMM Myer Centre. Courtesy of Mary MacTavish; The Granite Island chairlift, Victor Harbor. Alex Prichard/Flickr; Rowley Park, Adelaide's ace suburban motorsport venue. Courtesy of Noel O'Connor; Elephant cart pulled by Samorn at the Adelaide Zoo. Photo by News Ltd/Newspix; Author photo, courtesy of 5DN

PRINTER Everbest, China

This book is printed on paper using fibre supplied from plantation or sustainably managed forests.

All reasonable efforts were taken to obtain permission to use copyright material reproduced in this book, but in some cases copyright holders could not be traced. The author welcomes information in this regard.

The Advertiser